Kahoot!
QUIZ TIME
DINOSAURS

Written by
Rona Skene

Contents

Introduction

Which dinosaur had the longest neck or the smallest brain? Are they alive today? How many teeth did *T. rex* have? Test your dinosaur knowledge with these quizzes, packed with amazing facts about the incredible animals that stomped, crawled, flew, or swam on Earth millions of years ago.

Test yourself on the terrifying tyrannosaurs, stupendous sauropods, armored ankylosaurs, and ravenous raptors that ruled our prehistoric planet. Ready? Let's go on a dinosaur hunt!

Keep score

Most quizzes in this book have 10 questions each. To keep score, you'll need to record the number of correct answers each player gets after each quiz.

Keep track on a piece of paper or even on a spreadsheet. Be sure to tally up the score for each quiz in order to crown the ultimate winner based on who gets the highest score from all 30 quizzes. Who will grab the gold medal?

Find more quizzes!

Look for QR codes throughout the book. Scan them to find exclusive online quizzes on the same theme. You can also head over to www.kahoot.com to discover more than 100 million quizzes on lots of interesting subjects!

Find 15 QR codes like this one on the pages that follow.

Make your own

Once you've completed these quizzes, get inspired to create your own on kahoot.com!

First, plan out your questions on paper and check out our top tips to make your quiz the best it can be. When it's ready, share your quiz with friends and family.

Don't worry about who wins or if your quiz doesn't turn out exactly how you planned. The important thing is to have fun, but it's even more important to stay safe online. Never share any personal information with anyone online and always use the internet with a trusted adult.

Top tips

1 Do your research and always check your facts with three trusted online sources.

2 Give your quiz a fun theme and vary your questions so the quiz doesn't get repetitive.

3 Include three or four multiple choice options plus a few true or false and picture rounds.

Before Dinosaurs

Dinosaurs weren't the first creatures on Earth. Before them, other life forms floated, swam, crawled, or flew around our planet.

1 **When did life first appear on Earth?**
- ◆ 4.5 billion years ago
- ▲ 3.5 billion years ago
- ● 1 billion years ago

2 **These are living examples of the oldest fossils. Where are they?**
- ◆ Western Australia
- ▲ South Africa
- ● Northern Germany

3 **Which geological period saw the first "explosion" of new life forms in the ocean?**
- ◆ Precambrian
- ▲ Cambrian
- ● Ordovician

4 **What was unusual about the early fish called *Tiktaalik*?**
- ◆ It swam backward
- ▲ It had no eyes
- ● It could walk

Did you know?
All known fossils that we have found from the Cambrian Period are trilobites—small woodlouse lookalikes that crawled along the seabed.

5 The first forests on Earth were formed by which tree?

◆ *Archaeopteris*
▲ Archaeologist
● Archipelago

6 True or false: *Meganeura* was the biggest ever insect on Earth.

◆ True
▲ False

7 What did ammonites have on the outside of their bodies?

◆ A shell
▲ Scales
● Feathers

8 Which ancestor of today's sharks had a dorsal fin shaped like an ironing board?

◆ *Stethacanthus*
▲ *Dunkleosteus*
● *Sharkopteris*

9 True or false: *Dimetrodon* was the first dinosaur on Earth.

◆ True
▲ False

Scan the QR code for a Kahoot! about before dinosaurs.

Turn to page 8 for the answers!

Before Dinosaurs
Answers

1 **When did life first appear on Earth?**

▲ 3.5 billion years ago

A billion years after Earth formed, microscopic organisms called *cyanobacteria* (below) emerged in water.

2 **These are living examples of the oldest fossils. Where are they?**

◆ Western Australia

These 3.5 million-year-old mounds are called stromatolites—preserved old bacteria sandwiched between sand layers that have become rock.

3 **Which geological period saw the first "explosion" of new life forms in the ocean?**

▲ Cambrian

Around 530 million years ago, new animals suddenly appeared, including the first creatures with heads, legs, skeletons, and shells. It's known as the Cambrian Explosion.

4 **What was unusual about the early fish called *Tiktaalik*?**

● It could walk

Tiktaalik used its strong fins as legs, dragging itself out of the water and crawling onto land.

5

The first forests on Earth were formed by which tree?

◆ *Archaeopteris*

Archaeopteris appeared in the Devonian Period, around 400 million years ago. It grew in swampy land and was a kind of cross between a fern and a modern conifer tree.

6

True or false: *Meganeura* was the biggest ever insect on Earth.

◆ True

This pigeon-sized predator was a common sight in the skies 300 million years ago. It was a top hunter, feeding on other insects and lizards.

7

What did ammonites have on the outside of their bodies?

◆ A shell

Ammonites were close relatives of today's octopus and squid. Their beautiful, coiled fossil shells can be from 0.5 in (1 cm) to 10 ft (3 m) across!

8

Which ancestor of today's sharks had a dorsal fin shaped like an ironing board?

◆ *Stethacanthus*

This fish's flat-topped fin was covered in small spikes. Only males had this fin, and they probably used it to gain female attention.

9

True or false: *Dimetrodon* was the first dinosaur on Earth.

▲ False

Crocodile-sized *Dimetrodon*, from the Permian Period around 270 million years ago, looks like a dinosaur but was actually a synapsid—an ancestor of modern-day mammals.

Podium!

Bronze: 1–5 correct answers
Silver: 6–8 correct answers
Gold: 9–10 correct answers

Triassic Times

During the Triassic Period, our planet filled up with all kinds of new life. But what was Triassic Earth like? Let's find out.

1 **True or false: The first dinosaurs appeared in the Triassic Period.**
- ◆ True
- ▲ False

2 **During the Triassic Period, how many continents were there on Earth?**
- ◆ One
- ▲ Three
- ● Seven

Did you know?
Carnivorous dinosaurs walked on two legs because it made them faster for chasing prey. Herbivores stood on four legs because they had a big, plant-digesting stomach to support.

3 **What was Earth's single ocean called?**
- ◆ Panthalassa
- ▲ Protopacific
- ● Paleoaquarium

4 **What was the Triassic climate like?**
- ◆ Cold and icy
- ▲ Cool and rainy
- ● Hot and dry

5 **Which of these is NOT a Triassic dinosaur?**
- ◆ *Plateosaurus*
- ▲ *Herrerasaurus*
- ● *Stegosaurus*

6 What type of plant is this?

◆ Fern

▲ Foxglove

● Fig tree

7 Dinosaurs are often divided into two groups, according to the shape of ...?

◆ Their heads

▲ Their feet

● Their hips

9 How did dinosaurs have their young?

◆ They had live babies, like mammals

▲ They laid eggs on land, like reptiles

● They spawned in water, like amphibians

8 Put these Triassic dinosaurs in order of size, largest first:

◆ *Mussaurus*

▲ *Plateosaurus*

● *Pisanosaurus*

10 The early dinosaur *Eoraptor* weighed the same as ...?

◆ A human toddler

▲ An elephant

● A large dog

Turn to page 12 for the answers!

Triassic Times
Answers

1 **True or false: The first dinosaurs appeared in the Triassic Period.**

◆ True

The earliest known dinosaurs, which turned up halfway through the Triassic Period, were mostly small and were outnumbered by other reptiles.

2 **During the Triassic Period, how many continents were there on Earth?**

◆ One

Pangea was the single landmass on Earth. It was a huge continent in the middle of a single ocean. Pangea only began to break apart at the start of the Jurassic Period.

3 **What was Earth's single ocean called?**

◆ Panthalassa

Surrounding the supercontinent of Pangea was a vast ocean called Panthalassa.

5 **Which of these is NOT a Triassic dinosaur?**

● *Stegosaurus*

This elephant-sized herbivore first appeared on Earth in the Jurassic Period. Its name means "plated lizard" because it has bony back plates.

4 **What was the Triassic climate like?**

● Hot and dry

The center of Pangea was a huge desert, with average temperatures above 120°F (50°C).

6. What type of plant is this?

◆ Fern

Ferns were common in the Triassic, growing in swampy areas. They were a key food source for herbivores.

7. Dinosaurs are often divided into two groups, according to the shape of ...?

● Their hips

Ornithischian dinos had backward-pointing hip bones. Saurischian dinos had hip bones pointing in different directions.

8. Put these Triassic dinosaurs in order of size, largest first:

▲ *Plateosaurus*

◆ *Mussaurus*

● *Pisanosaurus*

Plateosaurus (pictured) was 25 ft (8 m) long, *Mussaurus* was 10 ft (3 m) long, and *Pisanosaurus* was only 3 ft (1 m) long.

9. How did dinosaurs have their young?

▲ They laid eggs on land, like reptiles

Dinosaur eggs came in many sizes and shapes. Some dinosaurs built nests and sat on the eggs to keep them warm, like birds do today.

10. The early dinosaur *Eoraptor* weighed the same as ...?

◆ A human toddler

One of the earliest dinosaurs, *Eoraptor* was small and agile. It lived in rocky deserts and ate lizards, small reptiles, and plants.

Podium!

Bronze: 1–5 correct answers

Silver: 6–8 correct answers

Gold: 9–10 correct answers

Jurassic Giants

In the Jurassic Period, dinosaurs became Earth's top bananas—and here's a big bunch of questions about them!

1 Which of these events happened in the Jurassic Period?
- ◆ The supercontinent Pangea began to break up
- ▲ The Moon was formed
- ● There was an Ice Age

2 After the Triassic Period, Earth's climate in the Jurassic became:
- ◆ Much colder
- ▲ Much milder
- ● Much wetter

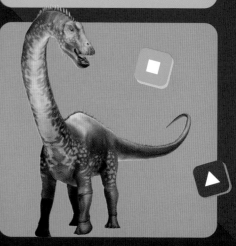

3 The largest plant-eaters, like this one, first appeared in the Jurassic. They were:
- ◆ Sauropods
- ▲ Ornithopods
- ● Theropods

Did you know?

Although the *Tyrannosaurus rex* was the star of the *Jurassic Park* movies, this deadly dinosaur did not actually appear until the start of the Cretaceous!

4 True or false: The biggest mammal in the Jurassic was the size of a horse.
- ◆ True
- ▲ False

5 What is a quadrupedal dinosaur?
◆ One that has four stomachs to digest plants
▲ One that walks on four legs
● One that lays square eggs

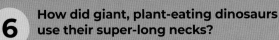

6 How did giant, plant-eating dinosaurs use their super-long necks?
◆ To headbutt carnivorous predators
▲ To reach the leaves of tall trees
● To watch for danger over tall grasses

7 Plant life changed in the Jurassic. The period is sometimes called:
◆ The Age of Cacti
▲ The Age of Cucumbers
● The Age of Cycads

8 True or false: We can't tell from fossils what color a dinosaur was.
◆ True
▲ False

9 What is the Jurassic Period named after?
◆ Jura Mountains, Switzerland
▲ Isle of Jura, Scotland
● Isaac Jurassky, fossil hunter

Scan the QR code for a Kahoot! about Jurassic giants.

10 True or false: The Jurassic Period ended with the extinction of the dinosaurs.
◆ True
▲ False

Turn to page 16 for the answers!

Jurassic Giants
Answers

1 Which of these events happened in the Jurassic Period?

◆ The supercontinent Pangea began to break up
Pangea split at first into two landmasses: Laurasia in Earth's Northern Hemisphere and Gondwana in the Southern Hemisphere.

2 After the Triassic Period, Earth's climate in the Jurassic became:

▲ Much milder

The breakup of Pangea meant that more land was close to the ocean, so conditions became cool and damp, making it much easier for life to thrive.

3 The largest plant-eaters, like this one, first appeared in the Jurassic. They were:

◆ Sauropods

These herbivores were the biggest animals to walk on Earth. With long necks and tails, they ate almost nonstop to fuel their huge bodies!

4 True or false: The biggest mammal in the Jurassic was the size of a horse.

▲ False

The biggest Jurassic mammals were as big as a beaver, but most were much smaller. Rat-sized *Sinoconodon*'s warm fur meant it could hunt at night, when it was too cold for dinosaurs.

5

What is a quadrupedal dinosaur?

▲ One that walks on four legs

Sauropods walked on four legs to support their big stomachs, which were needed to digest the huge amount of plant matter they ate.

6

How did giant, plant-eating dinosaurs use their super-long necks?

▲ To reach the leaves of tall trees

These Jurassic giants used their long necks to reach for food far and wide without having to move much.

7

Plant life changed in the Jurassic. The period is sometimes called:

● The Age of Cycads

Cycads look like palm trees, although they're from a different plant family. Conifers and ginkgo trees also became common.

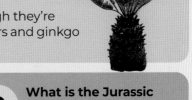

8

True or false: We can't tell from fossils what color a dinosaur was.

▲ False

Fossilized skin and feathers sometimes contain melanosomes—pigment cells. This tells us that dinosaurs came in a range of colors.

9

What is the Jurassic Period named after?

◆ Jura Mountains, Switzerland

The Jurassic Period was named after the area where the first Jurassic rocks were found in 1795.

10

True or false: The Jurassic Period ended with the extinction of the dinosaurs.

▲ False

The Jurassic extinction event killed off many ocean life forms, but it didn't have much effect on the dinosaurs.

Podium!

Bronze: 1–5 correct answers
Silver: 6–8 correct answers
Gold: 9–10 correct answers

Cretaceous Creatures

How did the dinosaurs go from heroes to zeros in 79 million years? Take this Cretaceous quiz and find out!

1 True or false:
The Cretaceous was the longest period of the Mesozoic Era.
- ◆ True
- ▲ False

2 What natural material is the Cretaceous named after?
- ◆ Iron
- ▲ Coal
- ● Chalk

3 Which Cretaceous creature is this a detail of?
- ◆ *Corythosaurus*
- ▲ *Troodon*
- ● *Triceratops*

Did you know?
During the Cretaceous, dinosaurs lived around the North and South Poles, which were free of ice and covered in thick forest.

4 Which type of plants first appeared in the Cretaceous?
- ◆ Flowering plants
- ▲ Carnivorous plants
- ● Underwater plants

5 True or false:
During the Cretaceous,
Earth's landmasses
formed a single
supercontinent.
◆ True
▲ False

6 Which huge
Cretaceous fossil site
is in Montana?
◆ Hell Creek
▲ La Brea Tar Pits
● Ghost Ranch

7 What is the name
of this relative of
Tyrannosaurus rex?
◆ *Arthurosaurus*
▲ *Alfredosaurus*
● *Albertosaurus*

8 The hadrosaurs
were named
for their ...?
◆ Bony heads
▲ Bulky bodies
● Ducklike
beaks

9 What event
ended both the
Cretaceous Period
and the dinosaurs?
◆ An asteroid strike
▲ A fast-spreading virus
● Massive flooding

**Turn to page 20 for
the answers!**

Cretaceous Creatures
Answers

1 **True or false:**
The Cretaceous was the longest period of the Mesozoic Era.

◆ True

The Mesozoic Era was the Age of the Dinosaurs, and the Cretaceous was its final period. Lasting for 79 million years, it was also its longest.

2 **What natural material is the Cretaceous named after?**

● Chalk

The word *creta* is Latin for chalk, and the Cretaceous was named by a Belgian geologist after the chalky rock layers laid down in Western Europe.

3 **Which Cretaceous creature is this a detail of?**

◆ *Corythosaurus*

This huge herbivore's name means "helmet lizard." The hollow crest on its head looked like the helmets worn by ancient Greek soldiers.

4 **Which type of plants first appeared in the Cretaceous?**

◆ Flowering plants

We can tell from fossils that the Cretaceous world was full of flowers and insects pollinating all the new plants.

5 True or false:
During the Cretaceous, Earth's landmasses formed a single supercontinent.

▲ False

In fact, the continents divided even more: Laurasia became Eurasia and North America, and Gondwana split into South America and Africa.

7 What is the name of this relative of *Tyrannosaurus rex*?

● *Albertosaurus*

Smaller than its famous relative, *Albertosaurus* was still a ferocious hunter with its huge jaws and jagged, banana-shaped teeth.

6 Which huge Cretaceous fossil site is in Montana?

◆ Hell Creek

During the Cretaceous, Hell Creek was a ridge on the shore of a shallow sea. Thousands of dinosaur fossils have been found here, including the first *Tyrannosaurus rex*.

8 The hadrosaurs were named for their ...?

▲ Bulky bodies

Hadrosaur means "bulky lizard." But these dinosaurs are also known for ducklike beaks used for clipping tough leaves.

9 What event ended both the Cretaceous Period and the dinosaurs?

◆ An asteroid strike

When an 8-mile- (13-km-) wide asteroid crashed into Earth, it raised a cloud of dust so thick that it blocked the Sun. First, the plants died, followed by the plant-eating animals, then the meat-eaters.

Podium!

Bronze: 1–5 correct answers
Silver: 6–8 correct answers
Gold: 9–10 correct answers

Theropods

Time to get up close and personal with some meat-munchers. But maybe not too close, and definitely not too personal!

1 How many legs did theropods use to move around?
- ◆ One
- ▲ Two
- ● Four

2 True or false: All meat-eating dinosaurs were theropods.
- ◆ True
- ▲ False

3 During which period did the first theropods appear?
- ◆ Triassic
- ▲ Jurassic
- ● Cretaceous

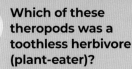

Did you know?

Some scientists think *Troodon* was the most intelligent dinosaur ever because it had the biggest brain relative to the size of its body. It may have used its brainpower to hunt in packs for bigger animals.

4 Which of these theropods was a toothless herbivore (plant-eater)?
- ◆ *Therizinosaurus*
- ▲ *Cryolophosaurus*
- ● *Troodon*

5 How many toes did theropods have on their legs?
- ◆ Two
- ▲ Four
- ● Five

6 Put these theropods in order of size, smallest first:
- ◆ *Velociraptor*
- ▲ *Microraptor*
- ● *Allosaurus*

7 Which fossilized body part of *Baryonyx* is this?
- ◆ Nose horn
- ▲ Thumb claw
- ● Tooth

8 *Citipati* fossils have been found in which desert?
- ◆ Atacama, Chile
- ▲ Sonora, California
- ● Gobi, Mongolia

9 True or false: *Tyrannosaurus rex* was the biggest theropod of all.
- ◆ True
- ▲ False

Scan the QR code for a Kahoot! about theropods.

10 Which group of theropods is still around today?
- ◆ Meerkats
- ▲ Lizards
- ● Birds

Turn to page 24 for the answers!

Theropods
Answers

1 **How many legs did theropods use to move around?**

▲ Two

Theropods walked and ran upright on their two legs. They used their arms to grab prey.

2 **True or false: All meat-eating dinosaurs were theropods.**

◆ True

Every carnivorous dinosaur scientists have found so far is a member of the theropod group.

3 **During which period did the first theropods appear?**

◆ Triassic

The first theropods (such as *Herrerasaurus*) appeared during the Triassic, about 230 million years ago. They were fast hunters.

4 **Which of these theropods was a toothless herbivore (plant-eater)?**

◆ *Therizinosaurus*

This theropod holds the record for the longest claws of any animal ever. It probably used them to pull down tree branches so it could eat the leaves.

5 **How many toes did theropods have on their legs?**

▲ Four

Theropods had three big front toes, plus one much smaller one at the back. They ran on the tips of their strong, widely spaced front toes.

6 Put these theropods in order of size, smallest first:

▲ *Microraptor*

◆ *Velociraptor*

● *Allosaurus*

Tiny predator *Microraptor* was the size of a modern crow, *Velociraptor* was 6 ft (1.8 m) long, and *Allosaurus* was 30 ft (9 m).

7 Which fossilized body part of *Baryonyx* is this?

▲ Thumb claw

Baryonyx means "heavy claw." This fish-eating theropod used its long, curved thumb claw to stab and snatch fish from the water.

8 *Citipati* fossils have been found in which desert?

● Gobi, Mongolia

These theropods were about the size of a modern emu. Females used their feathery arms to warm their eggs.

9 True or false: *Tyrannosaurus rex* was the biggest theropod of all.

▲ False

At 52 ft (16 m), *Spinosaurus* (pictured) was longer than *T. rex*. Only a few *Spinosaurus* bones have been found, so scientists are still learning about the biggest meat-eater yet discovered.

10 Which group of theropods is still around today?

● Birds

That robin outside is a relative of *Tyrannosaurus rex*! Scientists think that, like birds, most Cretaceous theropods had feathers.

Podium!

Bronze: 1–5 correct answers

Silver: 6–8 correct answers

Gold: 9–10 correct answers

Terrible Tyrannosaurs

Take the tyrannosaur test and see what you know about the biggest, most bloodthirsty predator that ever stomped Earth.

1 **During which period did *T. rex* first appear?**
- ◆ Triassic
- ▲ Jurassic
- ● Cretaceous

2 **How much did an adult *T. rex* weigh?**
- ◆ 1.1 tons (1 tonne)
- ▲ 3.3 tons (3 tonnes)
- ● 7.7 tons (7 tonnes)

3 **How many teeth did *T. rex* have?**
- ◆ 60
- ▲ 140
- ● 200

Did you know?

Scientists think that *T. rex* had a better sense of smell than other carnivorous dinosaurs, helping it sniff out prey in the dark.

4 **How long was *Tyrannosaurus rex*?**
- ◆ 13 ft (4 m)
- ▲ 39 ft (12 m)
- ● 82 ft (25 m)

5 True or false:
T. rex had the strongest bite of any land animal.
◆ True
▲ False

6 How much meat did *T. rex* need to eat each day?
◆ 200 lb (90 kg)
▲ 300 lb (136 kg)
● 400 lb (180 kg)

9 How long could *T. rex* live?
◆ Probably up to 28 years
▲ Probably up to 64 years
● Probably up to 92 years

10 What does the name *Tyrannosaurus rex* mean?
◆ Tyrant lizard king
▲ Ancient dinosaur god
● Terrifying hunting monster

7 What is this *T. rex*'s name?
◆ Drew
▲ Sue
● Wu

8 In which continent did *T. rex* live?
◆ Asia
▲ Europe
● North America

Scan the QR code for a Kahoot! about terrible tyrannosaurs.

Turn to page 28 for the answers!

Terrible Tyrannosaurs

Answers

1 **During which period did *T. rex* first appear?**

● Cretaceous

About 66–68 million years ago, *T. rex* made its appearance. It was one of the last of the giant dinosaurs that roamed Earth.

2 **How much did an adult *T. rex* weigh?**

● 7.7 tons (7 tonnes)

A fully grown *T. rex* weighed the same as a modern African elephant. This huge, bulky dinosaur probably hunted in short bursts of speed.

3 **How many teeth did *T. rex* have?**

◆ 60

The enormous, cone-shaped teeth were strong enough to bite bones in half. If a tooth broke, a new one replaced it.

4 **How long was *Tyrannosaurus rex*?**

▲ 39 ft (12 m)

From head to tail, *T. rex* was the length of a bus! When it moved, it held its long, stiff tail straight. This helped it balance its heavy head.

5 **True or false: *T. rex* had the strongest bite of any land animal.**

◆ True

It could bite with 7,937 lb (3,600 kg) of force—compare that to human jaws, which can only manage a mere 170 lb (77 kg)!

6 **How much meat did *T. rex* need to eat each day?**

▲ 300 lb (136 kg)

To have enough energy to hunt, supersized *T. rex* needed to eat the equivalent of 1,200 quarter-pounder burgers every day.

7 **What is this *T. rex*'s name?**

▲ Sue

Named after the fossil hunter who found the bones, "Sue" was discovered in 1990. In spite of her name, scientists don't know for sure that she was female!

8 **In which continent did *T. rex* live?**

● North America

Paleontologists have found most fossils in the northwest of the continent. *T. rex* hunted in the forests of the late Cretaceous.

9 **How long could *T. rex* live?**

◆ Probably up to 28 years

Scientists can tell from fossil bones that *T. rex* grew quickly, was fully grown as a teenager, and died quite young. The oldest tyrannosaur found was around 28.

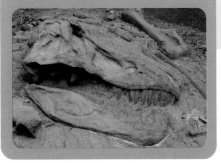

10 **What does the name *Tyrannosaurus rex* mean?**

◆ Tyrant lizard king

The first *T. rex* fossil was named by Henry Fairfield Osborn from the American Museum of Natural History.

Podium!

Bronze: 1–5 correct answers

Silver: 6–8 correct answers

Gold: 9–10 correct answers

Sauropods

Were sauropods the biggest, bulkiest creatures ever to stomp the Earth? Let's weigh the evidence ...

1 **What is the biggest sauropod found so far?**
◆ *Diplodocus*
▲ *Brontosaurus*
● *Argentinosaurus*

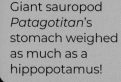

2 **The biggest sauropods were known as ...?**
◆ Titanosaurs
▲ Gargantosaurs
● Humongosaurs

3 **What does the name "sauropod" mean?**
◆ Sore-foot
▲ Bird-foot
● Lizard-foot

Did you know?

Giant sauropod *Patagotitan*'s stomach weighed as much as a hippopotamus!

4 **True or false: Sauropods' main food was smaller dinosaurs.**
◆ True
▲ False

5 **Which sauropod was named after an African mammal?**
◆ *Meerkatosaurus*
▲ *Cheetasaurus*
● *Giraffatitan*

6 True or false: *Supersaurus* was longer than a tennis court.

◆ True
▲ False

7 Which dinosaurs had the smallest brains?

◆ Theropods
▲ Sauropods
● Ceratopsians

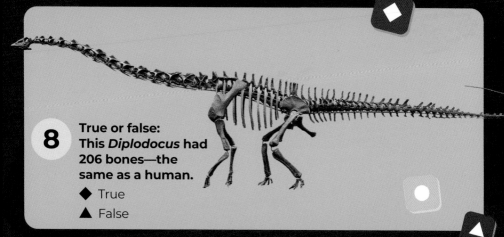

8 True or false: This *Diplodocus* had 206 bones—the same as a human.

◆ True
▲ False

9 Put these sauropods in order, from smallest to biggest:

◆ *Saltasaurus*
▲ *Camarasaurus*
● *Magyarosaurus*

Scan the QR code for a Kahoot! about sauropods.

10 True or false: Sauropods lived together in herds.

◆ True
▲ False

Turn to page 32 for the answers!

Sauropods
Answers

1 What is the biggest sauropod found so far?

● *Argentinosaurus*

So far, only fragments of this giant have been found, but it may have weighed 77 tons (70 tonnes)—as much as 38 family cars!

2 The biggest sauropods were known as ...?

◆ Titanosaurs

This group includes the colossal *Dreadnoughtus* and *Patagotitan mayorum*, which were both found in South America.

3 What does the name "sauropod" mean?

● Lizard-foot

Like other dinosaur names, this one is a bit confusing because sauropod footprints look more like a bear's than a lizard's!

4 True or false: Sauropods' main food was smaller dinosaurs.

▲ False

Sauropods were strict vegetarians. They grazed on leaves, branches, bark, and other plants.

5 Which sauropod was named after an African mammal?

● *Giraffatitan*

Like a giraffe, this skyscraping sauropod lived in Africa and used its mega-long neck to reach leaves on the tallest trees.

6 **True or false:**
Supersaurus **was longer than a tennis court.**

◆ True

This swamp-loving giant measured up to 108 ft (33 m) from snout to tail, whereas a tennis court is only 78 ft (24 m).

7 **Which dinosaurs had the smallest brains?**

▲ Sauropods

Compared to humans, all dinosaurs had small brains, but sauropods had the smallest of all in relation to their huge bodies.

8 **True or false:**
This *Diplodocus* **had 206 bones—the same as a human.**

▲ False

Diplodocus, with its very long neck and even longer tail, had many more bones than us— 356 in total.

9 **Put the sauropods in order, from smallest to biggest:**

● *Magyarosaurus* 20 ft (6 m)

◆ *Saltasaurus* 33 ft (10 m)

▲ *Camarasaurus* 59 ft (18 m)

Magyarosaurus was one of the smallest sauropods found so far and one of the last to appear, which it did in the late Cretaceous.

10 **True or false:**
Sauropods lived together in herds.

◆ True

Fossilized footprints, called trackways, show that sauropods moved in groups. One trackway shows 23 sauropods traveling together.

Podium!
Bronze: 1–5 correct answers
Silver: 6–8 correct answers
Gold: 9–10 correct answers

Ankylosaurs

The armored tanks of the Mesozoic were the ankylosaurs. What secrets were they hiding behind those tough shields?

1 True or false:
Ankylosaurus was the biggest of the ankylosaurs.
◆ True
▲ False

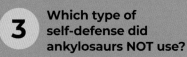

2 Which part of *Ankylosaurus* was NOT armor-plated?
◆ Eyelids
▲ Belly
● Neck

3 Which type of self-defense did ankylosaurs NOT use?
◆ Spikes
▲ Tail club
● Venomous bite

4 What does "ankylosaur" mean?
◆ Lizard with ankles
▲ Crooked lizard
● Tank lizard

5 What did ankylosaurs eat?
◆ Fish
▲ Small mammals
● Plants

Did you know?

Not even a *Tyrannosaurus* bite—the most powerful in history—was strong enough to get through *Ankylosaurus*'s armor!

6 Name this spiky ankylosaur:

◆ *Gastonia*

▲ *Sauropelta*

● *Saichania*

7 The tail weapon of *Euoplocephalus* was made of ...?

◆ Muscle

▲ Ivory

● Bone

8 True or false: Ankylosaurs could run faster than humans.

◆ True

▲ False

9 Which modern armor-plated animal is this?

◆ Armadillo

▲ Pangolin

● Crocodile

10 *Minmi*, one of the smallest ankylosaurs, was discovered in ...?

◆ Australia

▲ Austria

● Argentina

Scan the QR code for a Kahoot! about ankylosaurs.

 Turn to page 36 for the answers!

Ankylosaurs Answers

1 **True or false:** *Ankylosaurus* **was the biggest of the ankylosaurs.**

◆ True

This Cretaceous heavyweight grew up to 23 ft (7 m) long and weighed more than three rhinoceroses!

2 **Which part of** *Ankylosaurus* **was NOT armor-plated?**

▲ Belly

The underside of *Ankylosaurus* was its only vulnerable spot, with no bony plates. Even its eyelids were protected by tough bone!

3 **Which type of self-defense did ankylosaurs NOT use?**

● Venomous bite

There's no fossil evidence—so far—that any dinosaurs were venomous.

4 **What does "ankylosaur" mean?**

▲ Crooked lizard

The Greek word *ankylos* describes ankylosaurs' outer bones, which were curved and fused together to make thick plates.

5 **What did ankylosaurs eat?**

● Plants

All those horns and spikes were never used by ankylosaurs to hunt other animals. Instead, they gathered up plants and leaves with their mouths.

6
Name this spiky ankylosaur:

▲ *Sauropelta*

Rows of lethal neck and shoulder spikes would have made this dinosaur a painful mouthful for any passing predators!

7
The tail weapon of *Euoplocephalus* was made of ...?

● Bone

The terrifying tail club was made of big bones, called osteoderms, that fused together and grew within the dinosaur's skin.

8
True or false: Ankylosaurs could run faster than humans.

▲ False

Scientists estimate these tanklike dinosaurs lumbered around at about 3 miles (5 km) an hour—which is walking pace for a human.

10
Minmi, one of the smallest ankylosaurs, was discovered in ...?

◆ Australia

We know from fossilized stomach remains that this Cretaceous dinosaur was a fruit-eater.

9
Which modern armor-plated animal is this?

● Crocodile

Reinforcing the scales on the back of this distant dinosaur relation are rows of bony plates called osteoderms.

Podium!

Bronze: 1–5 correct answers
Silver: 6–8 correct answers
Gold: 9–10 correct answers

Ornithopods

These plant-eaters were a varied bunch, but they had some things in common. See if you can work out what made them tick!

1 What does "ornithopod" mean?
- ◆ Cat-footed
- ▲ Bird-footed
- ● Cow-footed

2 True or false: All ornithopods walked on two legs.
- ◆ True
- ▲ False

3 Which ornithopods are sometimes called duck-billed dinosaurs?
- ◆ Hadrosaurs
- ▲ Lambeosaurinae
- ● Iguanodons

4 Which of these dinosaurs was not an ornithopod?
- ◆ *Camptosaurus*
- ▲ *Heterodontosaurus*
- ● *Parasaurolophus*

5 This ornithopod is named after which Australian town?
- ◆ Muttaburra
- ▲ Wollongong
- ● Wagga Wagga

6 What did *Corythosaurus* have on its head?

◆ Very hard feathers

▲ A spiked horn

● A big crest

8 This fossil is which part of a *Parasaurolophus*'s body?

◆ Skull

▲ Front leg

● Tail

7 The biggest ornithopod was ...?

◆ *Ouranosaurus*

▲ *Shantungosaurus*

● *Velociraptor*

9 *Lesothosaurus* is named after a place in ...?

◆ Oceania

▲ Africa

● Europe

Did you know?

In 1878, 30 almost complete *Iguanodon* skeletons were discovered in one Belgian coal mine.

10 The elephant-sized *Iguanodon* was armed with:

◆ Massive tusks

▲ Scissorlike teeth

● Sharp thumb spikes

Turn to page 40 for the answers!

Ornithopods
Answers

1 **What does "ornithopod" mean?**

▲ Bird-footed

This group of dinosaurs got their name from their three-toed, birdlike feet—although some early ornithopods had four toes!

2 **True or false: All ornithopods walked on two legs.**

▲ False

Most ornithopods stood on their two back legs, but the bigger ones, such as *Edmontosaurus*, walked on all four limbs.

3 **Which ornithopods are sometimes called duck-billed dinosaurs?**

◆ Hadrosaurs

These plant-munchers had broad, ducklike beaks that they used to clip leaves.

4 **Which of these dinosaurs was not an ornithopod?**

▲ *Heterodontosaurus*

Heterodontosaurus is a heterodontosaurid. It was once thought to be an ornithopod.

5 **This ornithopod is named after which Australian town?**

◆ Muttaburra

Muttaburrasaurus gets its name from the town in Queensland, where it was first discovered in 1963.

6

What did *Corythosaurus* have on its head?

● A big crest

The sail-shaped crest was hollow and connected to *Corythosaurus*'s nose, so it may have been used to make noises, like a trumpet!

7

The biggest ornithopod was ...?

▲ *Shantungosaurus*

This 50-ft (15-m) hefty herbivore probably moved in herds across the swamps and fields of China, munching plants and leaves.

8

This fossil is which part of *Parasaurolophus*'s body?

◆ Skull

This hadrosaur had a long, tube-shaped crest on its head. It may have acted like a megaphone to make its call louder.

9

***Lesothosaurus* is named after a place in ...?**

▲ Africa

This turkey-sized early ornithopod was first discovered in Lesotho, a country in southern Africa, in 1978.

10

The elephant-sized *Iguanodon* was armed with:

● Sharp thumb spikes

The 6-in (16-cm) spikes on each hand were used to fight off predators, but *Iguanodons* may have used them to break open nuts or seeds, too.

Podium!

Bronze: 1–5 correct answers

Silver: 6–8 correct answers

Gold: 9–10 correct answers

Sticking Together

Gather your wits to tackle these questions about the dinosaurs that preferred being part of the gang to solo living.

1 What's the word for a group of dinosaurs?

◆ Pride

▲ Troop

● Herd

2 Why would meat-eaters form herds?

◆ To find new territory

▲ To keep warm

● To hunt together

Did you know?

We know *Utahraptor* hunted in packs because in 2015, the fossils of more than SIX *Utahraptors* and their plant-eating prey were found in one block of sandstone!

3 Which is NOT a reason for sauropods to form herds?

◆ To migrate to new feeding grounds

▲ To hunt for prey

● To protect each other

4 What do paleontologists call a line of dinosaur footprints in rock?

◆ A petrified path

▲ A fossil trackway

● A Triassic trail

5 Did *Velociraptors* hunt in packs?

◆ Yes

▲ Nobody knows for sure

● No

6 True or false: Dinosaurs migrated over long distances.

◆ True

▲ False

7 How long are the biggest dinosaur footprints ever found?

◆ 3.3 ft (1 m)

▲ 5.6 ft (1.7 m)

● 8 ft (2.4 m)

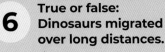
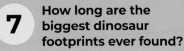

8 Why did *Maiasaura* form herds in Montana?

◆ To lay their eggs

▲ To migrate from the US to Canada

● To defend their food source

9 What does the name *Maiasaura* mean?

◆ Burrowing lizard

▲ Good mother lizard

● Mouse lizard

10 In a dinosaur herd, where did the babies go?

◆ At the back

▲ At the front

● In the middle

 Turn to page 44 for the answers!

Sticking Together

Answers

1 **What's the word for a group of dinosaurs?**
● Herd
Most scientists stick to "herd" to describe dinosaur groups, although you might read about a "flock" if the dinosaurs are especially birdlike!

2 **Why would meat-eaters form herds?**
● To hunt together
Some predators, such as *Deinonychus*, worked together to bring down much bigger prey. Carnivores that hunted in packs were the most intelligent dinosaurs.

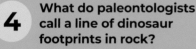

3 **Which is NOT a reason for sauropods to form herds?**
▲ To hunt for prey
Sauropods were plant-eaters. Living in herds helped keep them safe from predators.

4 **What do paleontologists call a line of dinosaur footprints in rock?**
▲ A fossil trackway
These fossilized tracks can show us where dinosaur groups were moving in the same direction together.

5 Did *Velociraptors* hunt in packs?

▲ Nobody knows for sure

Some evidence suggests they were solo hunters; other indications point to *Velociraptors* hunting in packs.

6 True or false: Dinosaurs migrated over long distances.

◆ True

Some fossil trackways are "superhighways," showing that dinosaurs traveled miles for food or to escape cold winters.

7 How long are the biggest dinosaur footprints ever found?

▲ 5.6 ft (1.7 m)

The massive tracks were left by giant sauropods on a trackway in western Australia.

8 Why did *Maiasaura* form herds in Montana?

◆ To lay their eggs

Hundreds of fossilized nests, all close together, tell us that *Maiasaura* came together to lay their eggs and raise their babies as a group.

9 What does the name *Maiasaura* mean?

▲ Good mother lizard

After they hatched, baby *Maiasaura* stayed safe in the nest while the adults brought them plants and leaves to eat.

10 In a dinosaur herd, where did babies go?

● In the middle

Fossils show that sauropod herds kept the youngest dinosaurs in the center of the group to shield them from attacks.

Podium!

Bronze: 1–5 correct answers

Silver: 6–8 correct answers

Gold: 9–10 correct answers

Ceratopsians

Meet the family of spectacular dinosaurs famous for their huge bony heads, pointed horns, and some very fancy neckwear!

1 What does "triceratops" mean?
- ◆ Three-toed feet
- ▲ Three-horned face
- ■ Armored lizard

2 What did *Triceratops* eat?
- ◆ Other dinosaurs
- ▲ Plants and trees
- ■ A mixture of meat and plants

3 The largest ceratopsian found so far was named:
- ◆ *Megaceratops*
- ▲ *Nanoceratops*
- ● *Titanoceratops*

Did you know?

Teeth marks from *T. rex* have been found on fossilized *Triceratops* bones!

4 *Protoceratops* was the size of which modern animal?
- ▲ Cat
- ● Sheep
- ■ Elephant

5 How many teeth did *Triceratops* have?
- ▲ 800
- ◆ None
- ■ 200

6 *Psittacosaurus*, meaning "parrot lizard," was named for its ...?

◆ Ability to fly
▲ Loud squawk
■ Curved beak

7 What is a ceratopsian's dramatic bony neck structure called?

◆ Frill
▲ Shield
● Collar

8 This five-horned ceratopsian is a ...?

◆ *Pentaceratops*
▲ *Octoceratops*
● *Quadriceratops*

9 True or false: *Velociraptor* was the main predator of *Triceratops*.

▲ True
● False

10 Which period in history did the Ceratopsians NOT live in?

▲ Jurassic
● Triassic
■ Cretaceous

Scan the QR code for a Kahoot! about ceratopsians.

Turn to page 48 for the answers!

Ceratopsians
Answers

1 **What does "*Triceratops*" mean?**

▲ Three-horned face

This giant ceratopsian had a short horn on the end of its nose plus two long, sharp brow horns.

2 **What did *Triceratops* eat?**

▲ Plants and trees

Triceratops used its strong, curved beak to tear off chunks from low-growing ferns and palms.

3 **The largest ceratopsian found so far was named:**

● *Titanoceratops*

This giant had a skull around 8.5 ft (2.65 m) long—that's as tall as an ostrich, the world's tallest bird!

4 ***Protoceratops* was the size of which modern animal?**

● Sheep

Like sheep, these early ceratopsians lived in herds. This tactic made it harder for predators to hunt them.

5 **How many teeth did *Triceratops* have?**

▲ 800

Rows of tightly packed, scissorlike teeth moved upward like conveyor belts, replacing teeth that were quickly worn down from chomping tough leaves.

6 *Psittacosaurus,* meaning "parrot lizard," was named for its ...?

■ Curved beak

Like all ceratopsians, this little dinosaur had a birdlike beak made of keratin, the same material as in modern bird beaks.

7 What is a ceratopsian's dramatic bony neck structure called?

◆ Frill

These plates of solid bone continued to grow throughout the animal's lifetime. They were probably used for self-defense and as a display to impress potential mates.

8 This five-horned ceratopsian is a ...?

◆ *Pentaceratops*

Pentaceratops actually only had three "real" horns—the other two, on the sides of its face, are actually pointed cheek bones.

9 True or false: *Velociraptor* was the main predator of *Triceratops.*

● False

Velociraptors were alive before the time of *Triceratops.* However, they did prey on *Protoceratops,* an earlier ceratopsian. *Triceratops'* major enemy was the carnivore *T. rex.*

10 Which period in history did the Ceratopsians NOT live in?

● Triassic

The Cretaceous was the peak time for dinosaurs on Earth, when they spread to every part of the globe.

Podium!

Bronze: 1–5 correct answers
Silver: 6–8 correct answers
Gold: 9–10 correct answers

Mini Dinosaurs

Not all dinosaurs were as big as a house! Get a magnifying glass and investigate the miniature world of the dinkiest dinosaurs.

1 *Eoraptor*, one of the first dinosaurs, was the size of a ...?
◆ Mouse
▲ Fox
● Pony

2 One of the first full dinosaurs ever found, this fossil is a ...?
◆ *Minisauripus*
▲ *Compsognathus*
● *Anchiornis*

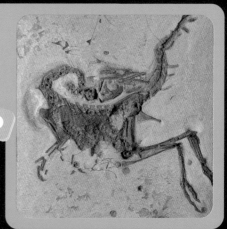

3 The name *Compsognathus* means:
◆ Fairy feet
▲ Small hands
● Dainty jaw

Did you know?

Microraptor had four "wings"—two on its arms and two on its legs!

4 *Dilong* was an unusually small member of which family of giants?
◆ Tyrannosaurs
▲ Sauropods
● Ceratopsians

5 What's the name of the rabbit-sized ancestor of *Triceratops*?

◆ *Bunnyhops*

▲ *Lapinops*

● *Aquilops*

6 Can you identify this small meat-eater?

◆ *Velociraptor*

▲ *Nanoraptor*

● *Microraptor*

7 One of the smallest sauropods, *Europasaurus*, was the size of ...?

◆ A squirrel

▲ A leopard

● A bull

8 The small armored dinosaur *Minmi* was an ...?

◆ Ankylosaur

▲ Tyrannosaur

● Titanosaur

Turn to page 52 for the answers!

9 What's the smallest dinosaur ever?

◆ *Microraptor*

▲ Bee hummingbird

● *Herrerasaurus*

10 Which mini raptor was named after a Disney character?

◆ *Nemoraptor*

▲ *Dumboraptor*

● *Bambiraptor*

Mini Dinosaurs
Answers

1 *Eoraptor*, one of the first dinosaurs, was the size of a ...?

▲ Fox

The first dinosaurs to appear on Earth were surprisingly small! *Eoraptor* was fast and agile and probably hunted like a fox, too!

2 One of the first full dinosaurs ever found, this fossil is a ...?

▲ *Compsognathus*

This turkey-sized, carnivorous theropod was uncovered in Germany in the late 1850s.

3 The name *Compsognathus* means:

● Dainty jaw

This hunter may have looked dainty, but its skeleton shows that it was a fast runner with ferociously sharp claws!

4 *Dilong* was an unusually small member of which family of giants?

◆ Tyrannosaurs

This Early Cretaceous carnivore looked a lot like its famous relative, *Tyrannosaurus rex*, except that it was only 5 ft (1.6 m) long!

5 What's the name of the rabbit-sized ancestor of *Triceratops*?

● *Aquilops*

This recently discovered dinosaur had the same curved beak as *Triceratops* but no bony "frill" around its skull.

6

Can you identify this small meat-eater?

● *Microraptor*

The *Microraptor* is one of the smallest dinosaurs found so far. It was the size of a crow, had lots of feathers, and could likely fly for short distances.

7

One of the smallest sauropods, *Europasaurus*, was the size of ...?

● A bull

In a family of supergiants, *Europasaurus* counts as little! Only one has ever been found, in a quarry in Germany.

8

The small armored dinosaur *Minmi* was an ...?

◆ Ankylosaur

We know that this 9.5-ft- (3-m-) long dinosaur ate fruit because a fossil was found with preserved stomach contents!

9

What's the smallest dinosaur ever?

▲ Bee hummingbird

Since most scientists agree that birds are dinosaurs, the smallest living bird, the bee hummingbird, is also the smallest dinosaur! This tiny bird weighs just 0.07 oz (2 g).

10

Which mini raptor was named after a Disney character?

● *Bambiraptor*

This very small but fierce hunter was discovered in 1994 by a 14-year-old fossil hunter in Glacier National Park, Montana.

Podium!

Bronze: 1–5 correct answers
Silver: 6–8 correct answers
Gold: 9–10 correct answers

Stegosaurs

Among the most famous Jurassic dinosaur families, Stegosaurs had a lethal weapon that deterred even the hungriest hunters!

1 **What did stegosaurs have on their backs?**
- ◆ Bony plates
- ▲ Fan-shaped crests
- ● Rows of spikes

2 **What does "stegosaur" mean?**
- ◆ Armored lizard
- ▲ Spiny lizard
- ● Roofed lizard

3 **How were *Stegosaurus*'s plates arranged?**
- ◆ In one straight line
- ▲ In two parallel rows

Did you know?
Fossilized bones of the predator *Allosaurus* show signs of serious wounds inflicted by spiky *Stegosaurus* tails!

4 **True or false: *Stegosaurus*'s plates were part of its spine.**
- ◆ True
- ▲ False

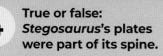

5 ***Stegosaurus* had a covering of extra-tough scales over its ...?**
- ◆ Throat
- ▲ Stomach
- ● Eyes

6 *Stegosaurus* was as big as ...?

◆ A cow
▲ An African elephant
● A house

7 *Stegosaurus*'s brain was ...?

◆ Apple-shaped
▲ Egg-shaped
● Banana-shaped

8 True or false: Stegosaurs had large, toothless beaks.

◆ True
▲ False

9 What was *Stegosaurus*'s main defensive weapon?

◆ Its back plates
▲ Its strong beak
● Its spiky tail

Scan the QR code for a Kahoot! about stegosaurs.

Turn to page 56 for the answers!

10 Which stegosaur had 40 bones in its tail?

◆ *Stegosaurus*
▲ *Kentrosaurus*
● *Huayangosaurus*

Stegosaurs
Answers

1 **What did stegosaurs have on their backs?**

◆ Bony plates

The biggest stegosaur, *Stegosaurus*, had between 17 and 22 huge, diamond-shaped plates running down its back.

2 **What does "stegosaur" mean?**

● Roofed lizard

The Greek word *stegos* means "roof." Fossil hunters chose the name because they thought the bony plates looked like roof tiles!

3 **How were *Stegosaurus*'s plates arranged?**

▲ In two parallel rows

The plates along the two rows were staggered in an alternating pattern—left plate, right plate.

4 **True or false: *Stegosaurus*'s plates were part of its spine.**

▲ False

The plates weren't part of *Stegosaurus*'s skeleton. They were bones embedded inside the skin, called osteoderms.

5 ***Stegosaurus* had a covering of extra-tough scales over its ...?**

◆ Throat

The scales protected *Stegosaurus*'s vulnerable throat from predators' teeth and claws. They were hard but flexible, so the dinosaur could still move its head.

6 *Stegosaurus* was as big as ...?

▲ An African elephant

African elephants are the biggest land animals today, but compared to some giant dinosaurs around at the same time, *Stegosaurus* was quite puny!

7 *Stegosaurus's* brain was ...?

● Banana-shaped

As well as having an odd shape, *Stegosaurus's* brain was very small—the same size as a dog's—compared to its huge body.

8 True or false: Stegosaurs had large, toothless beaks.

▲ False

Stegosaurs had beaks and teeth! They used their bony beaks for clipping leaves and twigs and their back teeth for slicing them up before swallowing.

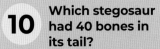

9 What was *Stegosaurus's* main defensive weapon?

● Its spiky tail

With its four long, lethal spikes, a blow from *Stegosaurus's* tail could inflict crippling wounds on its enemies.

10 Which stegosaur had 40 bones in its tail?

▲ *Kentrosaurus*

The extra bones made *Kentrosaurus's* tail much more flexible. It could be whipped at high speed, slamming its long spikes into an attacker with deadly effect.

Podium!

Bronze: 1–5 correct answers
Silver: 6–8 correct answers
Gold: 9–10 correct answers

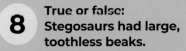

Skin, Scales, and Feathers

Who knew that some dinosaurs were so fluffy, feathery, and colorful? You did? Well, this quiz will be right up your alley!

1 True or false: Only bones can become fossils.
- ◆ True
- ▲ False

2 A dinosaur fossil with its skin still attached is called a ...?
- ◆ Skinny
- ▲ Mummy
- ● Wrinkly

3 What was dinosaur skin like?
- ◆ Scaly and waterproof
- ▲ Smooth and slimy
- ● Soft and wrinkly

Did you know?
Like a modern chicken, the Jurassic theropod *Juravenator* had a feathered body and bare, scaly legs.

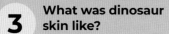

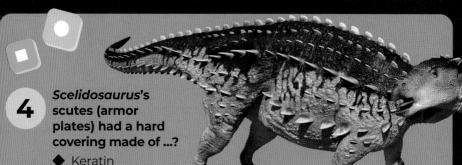

4 *Scelidosaurus*'s scutes (armor plates) had a hard covering made of ...?
- ◆ Keratin
- ▲ Gelatin
- ● Silicon

5 When did scientists find their first feathered dinosaur?

◆ 1866
▲ 1936
● 1996

6 The bumps on dinosaur skin where feathers sprout are called:

◆ Plume humps
▲ Quill knobs
● Down mounds

7 What type of feathers did *Anchiornis* have?

◆ Hollow and bristly
▲ Tufted and fluffy
● Long and smooth

8 Which substance in fossilized skin tells us a dinosaur's color?

◆ Collagen
▲ Melanin
● Indigo

9 Why did many smaller dinosaurs have fluffy feathers?

◆ To attract a mate
▲ To keep them warm
● To shield them from the Sun

10 *Psittacosaurus* had long bristles on its ...?

◆ Head
▲ Neck
● Tail

Turn to page 60 for the answers!

Skin, Scales, and Feathers
Answers

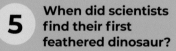

1 **True or false:**
Only bones can become fossils.

▲ False

Although there are more fossils of hard bones or teeth, soft tissue like skin can be fossilized, too, if the conditions around the remains are just right.

2 **A dinosaur fossil with its skin still attached is called a ...?**

▲ Mummy

This kind of preservation is valuable to scientists but very rare. Skin usually decays long before the fossilization process starts.

3 **What was dinosaur skin like?**

◆ Scaly and waterproof

Most dinosaurs had skin covered in scales, like a crocodile's or lizard's. Some had extra protection in the form of bony armor.

4 **_Scelidosaurus_'s scutes (armor plates) had a hard covering made of ...?**

◆ Keratin

This is a protein that toughens skin. It also forms hair, claws, hooves, and beaks.

5 **When did scientists find their first feathered dinosaur?**

● 1996

Found in China, the feathery _Sinosauropteryx_ changed science! Prior to this, it was thought dinos only had scaly skin.

6 **The bumps on dinosaur skin where feathers sprout are called:**

▲ Quill knobs

In 2007, scientists found quill knobs on a *Velociraptor* fossil—strong evidence that the predator had long arm feathers.

7 **What type of feathers did *Anchiornis* have?**

● Long and smooth

Like today's birds, dinosaurs had different feathers for different jobs. *Anchiornis*'s feathers were sleek, streamlined, and suitable for flying.

8 **Which substance in fossilized skin tells us a dinosaur's color?**

▲ Melanin

This pigment (natural skin coloring) is the same substance that darkens human skin to protect it from the Sun.

9 **Why did many smaller dinosaurs have fluffy feathers?**

▲ To keep them warm

Small animals lose heat more easily than bigger ones, so fluffy feathers are very useful to keep them warm.

10 ***Psittacosaurus* had long bristles on its ...?**

● Tail

This ceratopsian's tail had long, stiff bristles, like a porcupine's quills. It's possible that only males had these.

Podium!

Bronze: 1–5 correct answers

Silver: 6–8 correct answers

Gold: 9–10 correct answers

Ocean Dwellers

Dive into this quiz and find out how much you know about the different marine monsters of the Mesozoic!

1 True or false:
Some dinosaurs lived in the ocean.
◆ True
▲ False

2 Which of these is NOT a marine reptile group?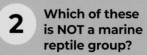
◆ Ichthyosaurs
▲ Plesiosaurs
● Hadrosaurs

Did you know?
The biggest fish was *Megalodon*, a prehistoric shark three times bigger than the great white shark!

3 True or false: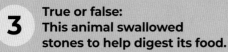
This animal swallowed stones to help digest its food.
◆ True
▲ False

4 *Ichthyosaurus* looked most like which modern ocean animal?
◆ Octopus
▲ Dolphin
● Walrus

5 Which marine reptile had more neck bones than any creature ever?
◆ *Angelonectes*
▲ *Alfredonectes*
● *Albertonectes*

6 Name this hulking ocean heavyweight:

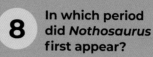

◆ *Pliosaurus*

▲ *Shonisaurus*

● *Lariosaurus*

7 What type of animal was *Archelon*?

◆ Jellyfish

▲ Turtle

● Shark

8 In which period did *Nothosaurus* first appear?

◆ Triassic

▲ Jurassic

● Cretaceous

9 The fierce predator *Mosasaurus* was named after:

◆ Moscow, Russia

▲ River Meuse, Holland

● Mozambique, Africa

10 True or false: The Loch Ness Monster is a surviving plesiosaur.

◆ True

▲ False

Scan the QR code for a Kahoot! about ocean dwellers.

Turn to page 64 for the answers!

Ocean Dwellers

Answers

1 **True or false: Some dinosaurs lived in the ocean.**

▲ False

Although dinosaurs could probably swim when necessary, they all lived on dry land. The oceans were the domain of different kinds of marine reptiles.

2 **Which of these is NOT a marine reptile group?**

● Hadrosaurs

They may have had bills like ducks, but these dinosaurs didn't live in the water!

4 **_Ichthyosaurus_ looked most like which modern ocean animal?**

▲ Dolphin

Looking like a cross between a dolphin and a swordfish, this marine reptile was perfectly adapted to chasing fast-swimming prey, like squid.

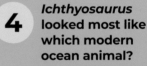

3 **True or false: This animal swallowed stones to help digest its food.**

◆ True

This is the plesiosaur _Elasmosaurus_. Like dinosaurs and modern birds, it used stones in its stomach to grind the food it ate.

5 Which marine reptile had more neck bones than any creature ever?

● *Albertonectes*

The long-necked plesiosaur *Albertonectes* had 76 vertebrae (neck bones). Giraffes only have seven!

6 Name this hulking ocean heavyweight:

◆ *Pliosaurus*

This plesiosaur ruled the seas in the Jurassic Period. With a skull longer than an adult man, it could bite and swallow prey bigger than a rhinoceros!

7 What type of animal was *Archelon*?

▲ Turtle

This ancient turtle was the largest of all time—over twice the size of today's biggest turtle, the leatherback.

8 In which period did *Nothosaurus* first appear?

◆ Triassic

Appearing 240 million years ago, crocodilelike *Nothosaurus* darted its head sideways to grab passing fish with its long teeth.

10 True or false: The Loch Ness Monster is a surviving plesiosaur.

▲ False

The dates don't add up! The loch is about 10,000 years old. The plesiosaurs went extinct 66 million years ago.

Podium!

Bronze: 1–5 correct answers

Silver: 6–8 correct answers

Gold: 9–10 correct answers

9 The fierce predator *Mosasaurus* was named after:

▲ River Meuse, Holland

Mosasaurus fossils were first discovered in the European river. It was 52 ft (16 m) long, making it one of the biggest ocean predators ever.

Pterosaurs

Is it a bird? Is it a plane? No, it's a pterosaur, and if it's heading your way, you'd better DUCK!

1 True or false:
Pterosaurs were dinosaurs that could fly.
◆ True
▲ False

2 **Pterosaurs were different from dinosaurs because they had ...?**
◆ Beaks
▲ Feathers
● Different skeletons

3 **Pterosaur wings were covered with ...?**
◆ Fluffy feathers
▲ Stretchy skin
● Waterproof scales

Did you know?
Pterosaurs' bodies were covered in pycnofibers—stringy structures that looked like fuzzy fur.

4 **Which of the following is true about *Dimorphodon*?**
◆ It could climb trees
▲ It was a plant-eater
● It could swim

5 What does **"*Dimorphodon*"** mean?
- ◆ Two-winged lizard
- ▲ Two kinds of teeth
- ● Two-clawed feet

6 True or false: On land, ***Pterodactylus*** walked on all fours.
- ◆ True
- ▲ False

8 This is the biggest flyer ever. Its name is ...?
- ◆ *Pterodactylus*
- ▲ *Quetzalcoatlus*
- ● *Rhamphorhynchus*

7 How did ***Rhamphorhynchus*** catch fish?
- ◆ It speared them with its beak
- ▲ It gripped them with its pointy teeth
- ● It scooped them into its pouch

9 ***Ornithocheirus*** had a bony crest on its ...?
- ◆ Tail
- ▲ Nose
- ● Head

Scan the QR code for a Kahoot! about pterosaurs.

10 Name this pterosaur from its silhouette.
- ◆ *Tropeognathus*
- ▲ *Eudimorphodon*
- ● *Pteranodon*

Turn to page 68 for the answers!

Pterosaurs
Answers

1 True or false:
Pterosaurs were
dinosaurs that
could fly.

▲ False

Pterosaurs were not
dinosaurs, although they
were closely related—
both were egg-laying
reptiles. These flying
animals ruled the skies
in the dinosaur age.

2 Pterosaurs were
different from
dinosaurs because
they had ...?

● Different
skeletons

Although pterosaurs
and dinosaurs would
have looked very similar
to us, internally their
hip and arm bones
were different.

3 Pterosaur wings
were covered with ...?

▲ Stretchy skin

Pterosaur wings
were made of thin,
featherless sheets of
leathery skin stretched
between their body
and their super-long
arm bones.

4 Which of the
following is true
about *Dimorphodon*?

◆ It could climb
trees

Dimorphodon wasn't
a very good flyer, but it
was a skilled climber and
scampered up trees like
a squirrel.

5 What does "*Dimorphodon*" mean?

▲ Two kinds of teeth

This pterosaur had long, sharp teeth in its upper
jaw and much smaller teeth in its lower jaw.

6 **True or false: On land, *Pterodactylus* walked on all fours.**

◆ True

Fossilized footprints show that when it walked, *Pterodactylus* folded up its wings and shuffled along, putting its weight on all four limbs.

7 **How did *Rhamphorhynchus* catch fish?**

▲ It gripped them with its pointy teeth

This Jurassic flyer hunted like a modern seagull. It swooped down to grab fish with its toothy beak.

8 **This is the biggest flyer ever. Its name is ...?**

▲ *Quetzalcoatlus*

This Cretaceous giant had a huge wingspan of 40 ft (12 m), the size of a big modern fighter jet!

9 ***Ornithocheirus* had a bony crest on its ...?**

▲ Nose

Like other pterosaurs, *Ornithocheirus* had hollow bones that were super-light— ideal for flying!

10 **Name this pterosaur from its silhouette.**

● *Pteranodon*

One of the most spectacular flyers ever, *Pteranodon* had a short tail, long legs, and a huge head. It had a long, pointy beak and an even longer, pointier crest on its head!

Podium!

Bronze: 1–5 correct answers
Silver: 6–8 correct answers
Gold: 9–10 correct answers

Hadrosaurs

Why not take a quack at this set of questions about those duck-billed dinosaurs we call the hadrosaurs?

1 True or false: Hadrosaurs had beaks and no teeth.
- ◆ True
- ▲ False

2 How did hadrosaurs use their teeth?
- ◆ To rip off chunks of meat
- ▲ To grind up tough leaves
- ● To tear bark from trees

3 What do hadrosaur fossils have more of than any other dinosaur fossils?
- ◆ Teeth
- ▲ Soft tissue
- ● Claws

4 A hadrosaur's back legs were ...?
- ◆ Longer than the front limbs
- ▲ Shorter than the front limbs
- ● The same length as the front limbs

Did you know?

Fossils have shown that some hadrosaur crests had colored stripes. These were probably used for display to attract potential mates.

5 How long was *Parasaurolophus*'s rodlike crest?
- ◆ 3.3 ft (1 m)
- ▲ 6 ft (1.8 m)
- ● 8.2 ft (2.5 m)

6 *Parasaurolophus* may have used its crest to ...?

◆ Shake fruit from trees

▲ Amplify the sound of its call

● Dig up plants to eat

7 Which duck-billed dinosaur is this?

◆ *Muttaburrasaurus*

▲ *Corythosaurus*

● *Parasaurolophus*

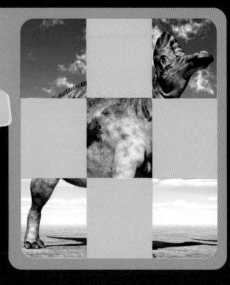

8 This fossil is of a hook-nosed hadrosaur called ...?

◆ *Gryposaurus*

▲ *Brachylophosaurus*

● *Lambeosaurus*

Scan the QR code for a Kahoot! about hadrosaurs.

9 True or false: *Muttaburrasaurus* had an inflatable nose.

◆ True

▲ False

Turn to page 72 for the answers!

Hadrosaurs
Answers

1 **True or false:**
Hadrosaurs had beaks and no teeth.

▲ False

Hadrosaurs had beaks as well as teeth, as you can see. They had more than 1,000 teeth in close-packed rows— more than any other dinosaurs.

2 **How did hadrosaurs use their teeth?**

▲ To grind up tough leaves

Hadrosaurs clipped leaves with their beaks, then used their back teeth to grind the foliage until it was soft enough to swallow.

3 **What do hadrosaur fossils have more of than any other dinosaur fossils?**

▲ Soft tissue

Nobody is sure why— maybe they had thicker skin that protected the tissues until the remains became rock.

4 **A hadrosaur's back legs were ...?**

◆ Longer than the front limbs

Their back legs were twice as long as the forelimbs and strong enough to let hadrosaurs stand upright to chomp on higher branches.

5 How long was *Parasaurolophus*'s rodlike crest?

▲ 6 ft (1.8 m)

That's long enough for an adult man to lie along it! The backward-facing crest was hollow, just like a tube, and joined up with the dinosaur's nostrils.

6 *Parasaurolophus* may have used its crest to ...?

▲ Amplify the sound of its call

The hollow crest may have acted a bit like a megaphone, allowing *Parasaurolophus* to communicate with the rest of its herd.

7 Which duck-billed dinosaur is this?

▲ *Corythosaurus*

The helmet-lizard giant! From the Greek *kranos*, meaning "helmet," and *sauros*, meaning "lizard."

8 This fossil is of a hook-nosed hadrosaur called ...?

◆ *Gryposaurus*

Males may have used their bulging beaks to butt and shove their rivals when tussling over a female mate.

9 True or false: *Muttaburrasaurus* had an inflatable nose.

◆ True—probably!

Most experts think *Muttaburrasaurus* pumped up air sacs in its nose to scare off rivals. One modern animal that can also pull off this trick is the hooded seal.

Podium!

Bronze: 1–5 correct answers

Silver: 6–8 correct answers

Gold: 9–10 correct answers

Fighting Back

Peaceful plant-eaters found ingenious ways to fend off hungry predators. Let's take a masterclass in dinosaur self-defense!

1 True or false: A sauropod's best weapon was its size.
- ◆ True
- ▲ False

Did you know?
Pachycephalosaurs' skulls were 20 times thicker than some other dinosaur skulls!

2 What kind of dinosaur was *Styracosaurus*?
- ◆ Hadrosaur
- ▲ Ceratopsian
- ● Stegosaur

3 Which of these dinosaurs used its tail as a club?
- ◆ *Euoplocephalus*
- ▲ *Apatosaurus*
- ● *Stegosaurus*

4 What would ankylosaurs NOT use their weapons for?
- ◆ Defending their territory
- ▲ Fighting rivals over a mate
- ● Bringing down prey

5 These tail spikes belong to ...?
- ◆ *Diplodocus*
- ▲ *Caudipteryx*
- ● *Stegosaurus*

6 Which giant probably used its tail as a whip?
- ◆ *Baryonyx*
- ▲ *Diplodocus*
- ● *Velociraptor*

7 Which dinosaur group's name means "thick-head lizards"?
- ◆ Pachycephalosaurs
- ▲ Plesiosaurs
- ● Parasaurs

8 Can you identify this long-clawed theropod?
- ◆ *Therizinosaurus*
- ▲ *Velociraptor*
- ● *Allosaurus*

9 Which dinosaur had an extra-long spike on each side?
- ◆ *Triceratops*
- ▲ *Kentrosaurus*
- ● *Gastonia*

Turn to page 76 for the answers!

Fighting Back

Answers

1 **True or false: A sauropod's best weapon was its size.**

◆ True

Giants like *Apatosaurus* could weigh over 44 tons (40 tonnes). They could crush a carnivore underfoot, so most predators stayed away!

2 **What kind of dinosaur was *Styracosaurus*?**

▲ Ceratopsian

Its horns, spikes, and frills look threatening, but a *Styracosaurus* probably only used them for display to impress mates and put off attackers.

3 **Which of these dinosaurs used its tail as a club?**

◆ *Euoplocephalus*

This armored ankylosaur's tail could deliver a blow powerful enough to stop a theropod in its tracks!

4 **What would ankylosaurs NOT use their weapons for?**

● Bringing down prey

Ankylosaurs ate plants. They used their weapons to defend themselves and their territory or to fight for a mate.

5 **These tail spikes belong to ...?**

● *Stegosaurus*

As well as their back plates, all stegosaurs had pairs of lethal spikes up to 3.3 ft (1 m) long at the end of their tails.

6 Which giant probably used its tail as a whip?

▲ *Diplodocus*

This huge sauropod probably used its incredibly long, slender tail to lash out at predators that got too close for comfort.

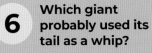

7 Which dinosaur group's name means "thick-head lizards"?

◆ Pachycephalosaurs

These dinosaurs' mega-thick, domed skulls were often crowned with a ring of stubby spikes. Unsurprisingly, their attack of choice was the head-butt!

8 Can you identify this long-clawed theropod?

◆ *Therizinosaurus*

Scissor-handed *Therizinosaurus* was a plant-eater, so it probably only used those huge 3.3-ft (1-m) claws to pull branches off trees.

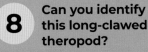

9 Which dinosaur had an extra-long spike on each side?

▲ *Kentrosaurus*

This was one of the spikiest of all the stegosaurs, making an attack from any direction a risky business for any hungry predator.

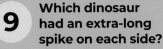

Podium!

Bronze: 1–5 correct answers
Silver: 6–8 correct answers
Gold: 9–10 correct answers

Dinosaur Detectives

Dig deep and uncover the truth about the people who tirelessly track down evidence of the Age of the Dinosaurs.

1 True or false:
In ancient Greece, people thought dinosaur bones came from aliens.
- ◆ True
- ▲ False

2 What does "dinosaur" mean?
- ◆ Big beast
- ▲ Terrible lizard
- ● Toothed animal

3 Who invented the word "dinosaur"?
- ◆ Julius Caesar
- ▲ Sir Richard Owen
- ● Sir David Attenborough

4 When was the first full dinosaur skeleton discovered?
- ◆ 1672
- ▲ 1756
- ● 1858

5 Where did Mary Anning, the first famous fossil-finder, make her discoveries?
- ◆ England
- ▲ US
- ● Kenya

6 Mary Anning discovered the first full skeleton of this marine reptile. What is it?

◆ Plesiosaur

▲ Ichthyosaur

● Mosasaur

7 Which two US fossil hunters had their own "Bone Wars"?

◆ Marsh and Cope

▲ Goodhall and Leakey

● Laurel and Hardy

Did you know?
When Mary Anning discovered the first Ichthyosaur skeleton, she was only 12 years old!

8 Marsh and Cope became enemies when Marsh ...

◆ Stole one of Cope's fossils

▲ Made fun of a skeleton Cope rebuilt

● Stood on a fossil and crushed it

10 What was paleontologist Jack Horner's biggest discovery?

◆ The world's oldest dinosaur footprint

▲ A graveyard of over 100 dinosaurs

● A group of 14 dinosaur nests

9 Who discovered the first *Tyrannosaurus rex* bones?

◆ Barnum Brown (US)

▲ Ringling Rogers (US)

● Chipperfield Clark (UK)

Turn to page 80 for the answers!

Dinosaur Detectives

Answers

1 True or false:
In ancient Greece,
people thought
dinosaur bones
came from aliens.

▲ False

Most thought the bones
were from mythical
creatures, like dragons.

2 What does
"dinosaur" mean?

▲ Terrible lizard

Dinosaur is made from
two Greek words: *deinos*,
meaning "terrible" or
"awesome," and *sauros*,
meaning "lizard."

3 Who invented the
word "dinosaur"?

▲ Sir Richard Owen

He worked at the Natural
History Museum in
London, UK, creating the
name in 1842.

4 When was the
first full dinosaur
skeleton discovered?

● 1858

The *Scelidosaurus* was
found in Dorset, England.
It was named "limbed
lizard" because of its
huge, pillarlike legs.

5 Where did Mary
Anning, the first
famous fossil-finder,
make her discoveries?

◆ England

Mary's finds were along the
UK coastlines of Dorset and
Devon. It's now known as the
Jurassic Coast.

6

Mary Anning discovered the first full skeleton of this marine reptile. What is it?

◆ Plesiosaur

When Mary first found the skeleton of this long-necked ocean reptile, some "experts" thought it was fake!

7

Which two US fossil hunters had their own "Bone Wars"?

◆ Marsh and Cope

Edward Drinker Cope and Othniel Charles Marsh became famous in the 19th century. They began as friends and colleagues but ended up falling out.

8

Marsh and Cope became enemies when Marsh ...

▲ Made fun of a skeleton Cope rebuilt

When Cope rebuilt an *Elasmosaurus* skeleton, he got its head and tail the wrong way around. Marsh pointed this out publicly—and an embarrassed Cope never forgave him!

9

Who discovered the first *Tyrannosaurus rex* bones?

◆ Barnum Brown (US)

Brown found the bones in 1902 in Hell Creek, Montana. In 1908, he found a more complete skeleton, which was used to make New York's famous *T. rex* exhibit.

10

What was paleontologist Jack Horner's biggest discovery?

● A group of 14 dinosaur nests

In Montana, Jack Horner and his team studied a cluster of *Maiasaura* nestsandeggs—evidence that these dinosaurs got together to lay eggs and raise their young.

Podium!

Bronze: 1–5 correct answers

Silver: 6–8 correct answers

Gold: 9–10 correct answers

Diplodocoids

Diplodocus was probably the longest land animal ever, and many of its relatives were almost as elongated!

1 True or false:
The diplodocoids were part of the sauropod group of dinosaurs.
- ◆ True
- ▲ False

2 Which of these sauropods is NOT a diplodocoid?
- ◆ *Apatosaurus*
- ▲ *Argentinosaurus*
- ● *Amphicoelias*

3 An adult *Diplodocus* was the length of ...?
- ◆ One bus
- ▲ Two buses
- ● Three buses

Did you know?
Diplodocus was one of the longest-living dinosaurs, reaching the age of 70–80 years old.

4 Which of these had the longest neck?
- ◆ *Dicraeosaurus*
- ▲ *Barosaurus*
- ● *Amargasaurus*

5 True or false: *Diplodocus*'s neck was longer than its tail.
◆ True
▲ False

6 What kind of habitat did diplodocoids live in?
◆ Meadows
▲ Tropical rainforest
● Wetland swamps

7 *Barosaurus* was as long as which sports playing area?
◆ Badminton court
▲ Basketball court
● Soccer field

8 The first *Diplodocus* skeleton was found in which US state?
◆ New Mexico
▲ Alaska
● Wyoming

9 *Nigersaurus* was first found in which continent?
◆ North America
▲ Oceania
● Africa

10 *Apatosaurus* weighed as much as ...?
◆ 1 elephant
▲ 4 elephants
● 10 elephants

Turn to page 84 for the answers!

Diplodocoids
Answers

1 True or false: The diplodocoids were part of the sauropod group of dinosaurs.

◆ True

Like all the sauropods, *Diplodocus* and family were huge plant-eaters that lumbered around on four thick legs.

2 Which of these sauropods is NOT a diplodocoid?

▲ *Argentinosaurus*

This giant was actually a member of the titanosaur group of sauropods.

3 An adult *Diplodocus* was the length of ...?

● Three buses

Diplodocus was the longest dinosaur of all. Despite its huge size, it was a bit of a lightweight, weighing only 11–16 tons (10–15 tonnes).

5 True or false: *Diplodocus*'s neck was longer than its tail.

▲ False

This giant's tail was longer than its long neck! The tail balanced out the dinosaur's weight, stopping it from tipping over when it leaned forward.

4 Which of these had the longest neck?

▲ *Barosaurus*

Its big, long neck was held up by 16 vertebrae (bones), some of which were more than 3.3 ft (1 m) long!

6

What kind of habitat did diplodocoids live in?

◆ Meadows

Diplodocoids preferred wide-open plains that had plenty of vegetation for them to eat. In the late Jurassic, North America provided the perfect habitat.

8

The first *Diplodocus* skeleton was found in which US state?

● Wyoming

In 1899, railway workers dug up an almost complete skeleton of *Diplodocus*. Casts were made of the skeleton and sent to museums all over the world.

7

***Barosaurus* was as long as which sports playing area?**

▲ Basketball court

An international basketball court is 90 ft (28 m) long.

9

***Nigersaurus* was first found in which continent?**

● Africa

This diplodocoid is named after Niger, the country in which it was found. *Nigersaurus* had a wide snout, which it used when eating grass.

10

***Apatosaurus* weighed as much as ...?**

▲ 4 elephants

Scientists think that, like an African elephant today, *Apatosaurus* used its bulk and strength to knock down trees so it could reach the tastiest, tallest branches.

Podium!

Bronze: 1–5 correct answers
Silver: 6–8 correct answers
Gold: 9–10 correct answers

Spinosaurs

Can you sail through these questions about spectacular African super-predator *Spinosaurus* and its family?

1 True or false: ***Tyrannosaurus rex* was bigger than *Spinosaurus*.**
◆ True
▲ False

2 **The first *Spinosaurus* fossil was found in ...?**
◆ South Africa
▲ Egypt
● Morocco

3 **Spinosaurs' heads were shaped like those of modern ...?**
◆ Spiders
▲ Crocodiles
● Snakes

4 **Spinosaurs spent some of their time in:**
◆ Swamps
▲ Deserts
● Forests

5 **A spinosaur's tall back crest is called a ...?**
◆ Fan
▲ Sail
● Arch

Did you know?

Spinosaurs died out around 93 million years ago, probably because the climate changed and many swamps dried up.

6 How did their sail help spinosaurs?

◆ It helped them run faster

▲ It kept them cool

● It helped them communicate

7 What was the sail definitely NOT used for?

◆ Attracting a mate

▲ Helping the spinosaur swim faster

● Trapping prey, like a net

8 Why was *Ichthyovenator* an unusual spinosaur?

◆ It had no sail

▲ It had two sails

● It had a triangular sail

9 Spinosaurs were tetanuran dinosaurs. What does this mean?

◆ They had no tongue

▲ They had stiff tails

● They had four claws on each foot

10 One the smallest spinosaurs found was called ...?

◆ *Irritator*

▲ *Innovator*

● *Indicator*

Scan the QR code for a Kahoot! about spinosaurs.

Turn to page 88 for the answers!

Spinosaurs
Answers

1 True or false: *Tyrannosaurus rex* was bigger than *Spinosaurus.*

▲ False

T. rex weighed 7.7 tons (7 tonnes), whereas *Spinosaurus* was longer and heavier. On land, *Spinosaurus* was the biggest predator ever.

2 The first *Spinosaurus* fossil was found in ...?

▲ Egypt

Paleontologists in Germany found part of a *Spinosaurus* skeleton at an oasis in the Egyptian desert in 1915.

3 Spinosaurs' heads were shaped like those of modern ...?

▲ Crocodiles

One spinosaur, *Suchomimus*, was given a name that means "mimicking a crocodile."

4 Spinosaurs spent some of their time in:

◆ Swamps

Spinosaurs probably nosed around in shallow water, looking for fish to eat in their long, narrow, toothy jaws.

5 A spinosaur's tall back crest is called a ...?

▲ Sail

Spinosaurus's huge sail was held up by bony spines. Some spines were around 6.5 ft (2 m) tall.

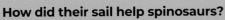

6 ▲ How did their sail help spinosaurs?

It kept them cool

Most scientists think that the sail, which was thin with a big surface area, was ideal for regulating temperature when conditions became too hot for comfort.

7 What was the sail definitely NOT used for?

● Trapping prey, like a net

As well as a swimming aid and a way to show off, the sail might also have been used as a warning to predators to stay away.

8 Why was *Ichthyovenator* an unusual spinosaur?

▲ It had two sails

Its sail had a split middle, dividing it in two. Its fossil was found in 2010 in Laos.

9 Spinosaurs were tetanuran dinosaurs. What does this mean?

▲ They had stiff tails

Scientists think this helped tetanurans keep their tails horizontal to improve their balance.

10 One the smallest spinosaurs found was called ...?

◆ *Irritator*

When a Brazilian fossil hunter found a new spinosaur, he repaired some missing pieces with plaster. Scientists were irritated when they found out ... hence the name!

Podium!

Bronze: 1–5 correct answers
Silver: 6–8 correct answers
Gold: 9–10 correct answers

Dinosaur Diets

From strictly vegan to mega-meat feasts, let's find out what's on the menu when dinosaurs dine out.

1 Which fossils tell us most about what dinosaurs ate?

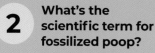

- ◆ Gut contents
- ▲ Dinosaur poop
- ● Bones

Did you know?

The biggest carnivore coprolite ever found is 26 in (67.5 cm) long and is in the Poozeum—a huge traveling exhibition of coprolites.

2 What's the scientific term for fossilized poop?

- ◆ Coprolite
- ▲ Dinodoo
- ● Excrelite

3 What do we call dinosaurs that eat both meat and plants?

- ◆ Varietovores
- ▲ Carnovegans
- ● Omnivores

4 What tells us that *Heterodontosaurus* was probably an omnivore?

- ◆ Nose
- ▲ Neck bones
- ● Teeth

5 True or false:
Dinosaurs used their
tongues a lot for eating.
- ◆ False
- ▲ We don't know
- ● True

6 What is
this *araucaria*
tree's common
name?
- ◆ Twisted
fir tree
- ▲ Monkey
puzzle tree
- ● Tortured
pine tree

7 What's the best
clue that a dinosaur
ate meat?
- ◆ Pointed teeth
- ▲ Long legs
- ● Huge stomach

8 True or false:
Iguanodon used its
huge thumb claw to
catch fish.
- ◆ True
- ▲ False

10 Name this long-
jawed, fish-eating
dinosaur.
- ◆ *Suchomimus*
- ▲ *Velociraptor*
- ● *Triceratops*

9 What was found
in an ichthyosaur
coprolite?
- ◆ Dinosaur bones
- ▲ Plants
- ● Hooks from the
arms of squid

 **Turn to page 92 for
the answers!**

Dinosaur Diets

Answers

1 Which fossils tell us most about what dinosaurs ate?

▲ Dinosaur poop

Gut contents are very rare, and bones do tell us some things, but fossilized poop reveals the most secrets about dinosaur diets!

2 What's the scientific term for fossilized poop?

◆ Coprolite

It's from the Greek *kapros*, meaning ... "poop!" If a coprolite contains seeds, bones, or fish scales, we know what the creature ate.

3 What do we call dinosaurs that eat both meat and plants?

● Omnivores

An omnivorous dinosaur might eat leaves, fruits, seeds, other dinosaurs, mammals, birds, fish, insects, and eggs. But not all at once!

4 What tells us that *Heterodontosaurus* was probably an omnivore?

● Teeth

It had different-shaped teeth: canines possibly for tearing meat, and flat cheek teeth for grinding plants.

5 True or false: Dinosaurs used their tongues a lot for eating.

▲ We don't know

Fossilized dinosaur tongues have not been found, so we don't know. It's likely that some dinosaurs used their tongues for eating.

6 What is this *araucaria* tree's common name?

▲ Monkey puzzle tree

This ancient tree is still around today. It was an important food source for plant-munching sauropods and many other herbivores.

7 What's the best clue that a dinosaur ate meat?

◆ Pointed teeth

Meat-eating dinosaurs (carnivores) had sharp, pointy teeth to tear into their prey.

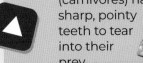

8 True or false: *Iguanodon* used its huge thumb claw to catch fish.

▲ False

Iguanodon's diet was plants only! It probably used its claw for self-defense or to tear down tree branches.

9 What was found in an ichthyosaur coprolite?

● Hooks from the arms of squid

Prehistoric squid called belemnites had 10 arms. These were covered in little hooks to grab prey with.

10 Name this long-jawed, fish-eating dinosaur.

◆ *Suchomimus*

It is a spinosaur. Another spinosaur, *Baryonyx*, was found with fish scales and a baby dinosaur in its stomach.

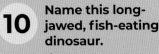

Podium!

Bronze: 1–5 correct answers

Silver: 6–8 correct answers

Gold: 9–10 correct answers

Raptors

Small, speedy, and seriously savage—meet *Velociraptor* and its ferocious family members!

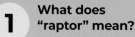

1 What does "raptor" mean?
- ◆ Runner
- ▲ Biter
- ● Grabber

2 When did raptors first appear?
- ◆ Triassic Period
- ▲ Jurassic Period
- ● Cretaceous Period

3 Which dinosaur family did raptors belong to?
- ◆ Dromaeosaurs
- ▲ Spinosaurs
- ● Tyrannosaurs

Did you know?

In 2018, footprints from a sparrow-sized raptor were discovered—evidence of the smallest nonbird dinosaur found so far!

4 True or false: Raptors were more intelligent than the average dinosaur.
- ◆ True
- ▲ False

5 Which secret weapon did raptors use to attack prey?
- ◆ Spiky tail
- ▲ Extra-long canines
- ● Rear claws

6 Put these raptors in size order, smallest to biggest:
◆ *Austroraptor*
▲ *Bambiraptor*
● *Velociraptor*

7 Why did raptors hold their rear claw off the ground?
◆ So they didn't trip over snakes
▲ So the claw stayed sharp
● So they could run faster

8 True or false: Raptors were excellent jumpers.
◆ True
▲ False

9 How fast could *Velociraptor* run?
◆ 25 mph (40 kph)— as fast as a human
▲ 40 mph (65 kph)— as fast as a tiger
● 75 mph (120 kph)— as fast as a cheetah

10 Raptors have been found everywhere except ...?
◆ Europe
▲ Antarctica
● Australia

Scan the QR code for a Kahoot! about raptors.

Turn to page 96 for the answers!

Raptors
Answers

1 What does "raptor" mean?

● Grabber

It's from the Latin word *raptare*, meaning "to grasp." Birds of prey, like eagles, are raptors, too, because they also seize their prey in talons.

2 When did raptors first appear?

▲ Jurassic Period

Raptors appeared toward the middle of the Jurassic. By the end of the Cretaceous, they had spread all over the world.

3 Which dinosaur family did raptors belong to?

◆ Dromaeosaurs

Fast-running dromaeosaurs were small but ferocious hunters. Most had long arms and large, sharp claws—ideal for pouncing on prey!

4 True or false: Raptors were more intelligent than the average dinosaur.

◆ True

Raptors had larger brains relative to their bodies than most dinosaurs—all the better for outwitting the prey they hunted.

5 Which secret weapon did raptors use to attack prey?

● Rear claws

Raptors had a long, curved, super-sharp claw on each hind leg. *Utahraptor*'s claws were 10 in (24 cm) long!

6. Put these raptors in size order, smallest to biggest:

▲ *Bambiraptor*

● *Velociraptor*

◆ *Austroraptor*

Most raptors were smaller than an adult human, but *Austroraptor* was up to 16 ft (5 m) long.

7. Why did raptors hold their rear claw off the ground?

▲ So the claw stayed sharp

Raptors used their razor-sharp, lethal rear claws to slash prey and pin it down.

8. True or false: Raptors were excellent jumpers.

◆ True

Dromaeosaurs had long, strong back legs. They could jump onto the backs of the big plant-eating dinosaurs they preyed on.

9. How fast could *Velociraptor* run?

▲ 40 mph (65 kph)— in short bursts

Velociraptor's body was light, lean, and muscular— built for speed instead of strength.

10. Raptors have been found everywhere except ...?

● Australia

Although fossils of other theropods have been found in Australia, no dromaeosaurs have been discovered—yet!

Podium!

Bronze: 1–5 correct answers

Silver: 6–8 correct answers

Gold: 9–10 correct answers

Eggs and Nests

Test your eggs-pertise with this brain-teasing quiz about Mesozoic moms and their babies!

1 True or false: All dinosaurs hatched from eggs.
- ◆ True
- ▲ False

2 Most dinosaur eggshells were ...?
- ◆ Soft and leathery
- ▲ Hard and brittle

3 The egg of *Apatosaurus* was as big as:
- ◆ A hen's egg
- ▲ An orange
- ● A basketball

4 Dinosaur nests were lined with:
- ◆ Feathers
- ▲ Scales
- ● Twigs and leaves

Did you know?

The biggest dinosaur egg found so far belonged to *Hypselosaurus*. A 12-in- (30-cm-) long egg was found in France in the 1960s!

5 True or false: Most dinosaurs built nests.
- ◆ True
- ▲ False

6 An egg from an unknown dinosaur species is called ...?

◆ A mystery egg
▲ A cryptova
● Oospecies

7 A *Maiasaura* nest contained ...?

◆ Up to 6 eggs
▲ Up to 20 eggs
● Up to 40 eggs

8 How big was a newly hatched *Maiasaura*?

◆ 8 in (21 cm)
▲ 10 in (25 cm)
● 12 in (30 cm)

9 How long did it take for the baby *Maiasaura* to double in size?

◆ 6 weeks
▲ 12 weeks
● 18 weeks

10 This is an egg from which dinosaur?

◆ *Triceratops*
▲ *Ankylosaurus*
● *Oviraptor*

Turn to page 100 for the answers!

Eggs and Nests

Answers

1 **True or false:
All dinosaurs hatched
from eggs.**

◆ True

As far as we know,
all dinosaurs laid
eggs, as do most of
today's reptiles.

2 **Most dinosaur
eggshells were ...?**

▲ Hard and brittle

Most dinosaurs laid
hard-shelled eggs, like
modern birds. A few
did lay soft eggs, like
those of today's snakes
and turtles.

3 **The egg of *Apatosaurus*
was as big as:**

● A basketball

This giant sauropod's
eggs were rounded, with
tough shells to protect
the embryos inside.

4 **Dinosaur nests
were lined with:**

● Twigs and leaves

Often, a dinosaur's nest
was built of sand, with
leaves and twigs added
to keep the eggs warm
and hidden from
predators' view.

5 True or false:
Most dinosaurs
built nests.

◆ True

Some dinosaurs made
nests above ground, but
most buried their eggs
underground, like
modern crocodiles do.

6 An egg from an
unknown dinosaur
species is called ...?

● Oospecies

Unless eggs are
found with the mother,
it's hard to identify the
species. Scientists give
these unknown eggs a
name: oospecies.

7 A *Maiasaura* nest
contained ...?

● Up to 40 eggs

Maiasaura laid 30–40
eggs in a circle. Each
one was the size of an
ostrich egg—about
8 in (21 cm) long.

9 How long did it
take for the baby
Maiasaura to double
in size?

◆ 6 weeks

Like all baby dinos,
Maiasaura grew fast—
it had to, to survive
predators. Within a
year, it would be 10 ft
(3 m) long.

8 How big was
a newly hatched
Maiasaura?

● 12 in (30 cm)

Maiasaura embryos
were curled up very tight
to fit inside their eggs.

Podium!

Bronze: 1–5 correct answers
Silver: 6–8 correct answers
Gold: 9–10 correct answers

10 This is an egg from
which dinosaur?

● *Oviraptor*

Scientists think the
female *Oviraptor* laid
more than 10 of these
sausage-shaped eggs,
then, like a bird today,
sat on the nest until they
hatched.

Dinosaur Neighbors

Dinosaurs may have ruled in Mesozoic times, but many other creatures were crawling, flying, and buzzing around, too!

1 When did the first mammals appear?
- ◆ Triassic Period
- ▲ Jurassic Period
- ● Cretaceous Period

Did you know?
The early mammal *Volaticotherium* could glide from tree to tree, just like today's flying squirrels!

2 Mammal ancestor *Robertia* is a member of which animal group?
- ◆ Sauropods
- ▲ Pterosaurs
- ● Therapsids

3 What is NOT true of most mammals?
- ◆ They have fur
- ▲ They produce milk for their babies
- ● They can replace teeth all their lives

4 True or false: Mammals developed fur as camouflage.
- ◆ True
- ▲ False

5 Most of the earliest mammals were the size of:
◆ Mice
▲ Cats
● Cows

6 We know that *Repenomamus* ate ...?
◆ Other mammals
▲ Baby dinosaurs
● Insects

7 Can you name this ratlike mammal?
◆ *Teinolophos*
▲ *Sinodelphys*
● *Zalambdalestes*

8 The first land animals on Earth were ...?
◆ Amphibians
▲ Insects
● Millipedes

9 Which insect pollinated Earth's first flowering plants?
◆ Bee
▲ Butterfly
● Beetle

10 True or false: Dinosaurs were pestered by flies.
◆ True
▲ False

Scan the QR code for a Kahoot! about dinosaur neighbors.

 Turn to page 104 for the answers!

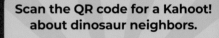
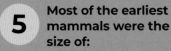
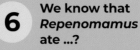

Dinosaur Neighbors

Answers

1 **When did the first mammals appear?**

◆ Triassic Period

Mammals appeared about 225 million years ago—almost at the start of the Age of the Dinosaurs.

2 **Mammal ancestor *Robertia* is a member of which animal group?**

● Therapsids

These creatures appeared in the Permian Period. *Robertia* was a cat-sized plant-eater.

3 **What is NOT true of most mammals?**

● They can replace teeth all their lives

Unlike most reptiles and fish, mammals replace their teeth only once. After the adult teeth come through, they're stuck with them!

4 **True or false: Mammals developed fur as camouflage.**

▲ False

Scientists think that fur was for warmth—it helped mammals hunt at night, when other predators were safely asleep!

5 **Most of the earliest mammals were the size of:**

◆ Mice

Most Triassic mammals were tiny, nocturnal animals, hiding in undergrowth or in underground burrows during the day.

6 We know that *Repenomamus* ate ...?

▲ Baby dinosaurs

A *Repenomamus* fossil was found with the remains of a baby dinosaur in its stomach!

7 Can you name this ratlike mammal?

● *Zalambdalestes*

With its long snout and flexible tail, *Zalambdalestes* looks like a rat, but true rodents did not appear until after the Mesozoic Era.

8 The first land animals on Earth were ...?

● Millipedes

These ancient arthropods have been crawling over Earth for 425 million years—more than 200 million years before the dinosaurs appeared!

9 Which insect pollinated Earth's first flowering plants?

● Beetle

The first beetles appeared before the Age of the Dinosaurs and long before bees and butterflies evolved.

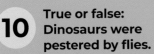

10 True or false: Dinosaurs were pestered by flies.

◆ True

Flies arrived at the same time as the dinosaurs. The flies targeted dinosaurs, biting them and sucking their blood.

Podium!

Bronze: 1–5 correct answers
Silver: 6–8 correct answers
Gold: 9–10 correct answers

Extinction

Around 66 million years ago, the dinosaurs had a very bad day. How much do you know about the dinosaurs' disappearance?

1 The disaster that ended the dinosaurs was called the ...?
- ◆ Ninth Ice Age
- ▲ Great Death
- ● Cretaceous Extinction Event

2 True or false: Meat-eating dinosaurs became extinct before the plant-eaters.
- ◆ True
- ▲ False

3 What happened after the meteor struck?
- ◆ There was a nuclear explosion
- ▲ Earth moved closer to the Sun
- ● A huge dust cloud formed

Did you know?

Two billion years ago, an even bigger meteor hit Earth. It landed in South Africa, leaving a crater 25 miles (40 km) deep!

4 In the Extinction Event, what percentage of living things died out?
- ◆ 50%
- ▲ 70%
- ● 90%

5 True or false:
The flying pterosaurs
survived and evolved
into birds.
- ◆ True
- ▲ False

6 Where on Earth
did the destructive
meteor land?
- ◆ Mexico
- ▲ Russia
- ● Scotland

7 What do scientists
call the extinction
event meteor?
- ◆ The Mexican
meteor
- ▲ The Chicxulub
impactor
- ● The Yucatán
terminator

8 True or false:
The Chicxulub
asteroid was the size
of Paris, France.
- ◆ True
- ▲ False

9 After Chicxulub,
how long did it take
for Earth's forests to
grow again?
- ◆ 10 years
- ▲ 1,000 years
- ● 100,000 years

10 The largest animal survivors of the disaster were ...?
- ◆ The size of
a shrew
- ▲ The size of
a dog
- ● The size of
a hippopotamus

Turn to page 108 for
the answers!

Extinction
Answers

1 **The disaster that ended the dinosaurs was called the …?**
- ● Cretaceous Extinction Event

The Cretaceous Period—and the nonbird dinosaurs—ended after a giant asteroid struck Earth 66 million years ago.

2 **True or false: Meat-eating dinosaurs became extinct before the plant-eaters.**
- ▲ False

With no plants to eat, the herbivores died out first. Then, with no prey to hunt, the carnivores followed into extinction.

3 **What happened after the meteor struck?**
- ● A huge dust cloud formed

The impact created so much dust that it blocked out the sunlight, killing off most plants.

4 **In the Extinction Event, what percentage of living things died out?**
- ▲ 70%

Almost three-quarters of plant and animal species were wiped out, making it one of the biggest extinction events ever.

5 **True or false: The flying pterosaurs survived and evolved into birds.**
- ▲ False

No pterosaurs survived the mass extinction, and they weren't related to birds. Some ground-living birds were able to survive though.

6 Where on Earth did the destructive meteor land?

◆ Mexico

In Yucatán in Mexico, the meteor's impact crater is 112 miles (180 km) wide. It is now buried deep underground and under the seabed.

7 What do scientists call the extinction event meteor?

▲ The Chicxulub impactor

The meteor is named after the Mexican town nearest to its impact site (pronounced "chick-soo-loob").

8 True or false: The Chicxulub asteroid was the size of Paris, France.

◆ True

The huge space rock measured about 6 miles (10 km) across. Some scientists think it was a broken-off piece of a comet deflected by Jupiter.

9 After Chicxulub, how long did it take for Earth's forests to grow again?

● 100,000 years

It took trees thousands of years to recover from Earth's three-year "impact winter," when there was very little light and extreme cold.

10 The largest animal survivors of the disaster were ...?

▲ The size of a dog

Mammals like this *Didelphodon* survived—in fact, the loss of their big predators was good news for them!

Podium!

Bronze: 1–5 correct answers
Silver: 6–8 correct answers
Gold: 9–10 correct answers

After the Dinosaurs

The end of the dinosaurs meant the beginning for some new animals. Can you tell a *Dromornis* from a *Diprotodon*?

1 When the Mesozoic Era ended, which era began?
- ◆ The Cenozoic Era
- ▲ The Ice Age Era
- ● The Stone Age Era

2 The Cenozoic Era is also called ...?
- ◆ The Age of Birds
- ▲ The Age of Reptiles
- ● The Age of Mammals

3 What is this saber-toothed cat's proper name?
- ◆ *Smilodon*
- ▲ *Andrewsarchus*
- ● *Arctodus*

4 How long were *Smilodon*'s two canine teeth?
- ◆ 4 in (10 cm)
- ▲ 5.5 in (14 cm)
- ● 7 in (18 cm)

5 What kind of animal was *Arctodus*?
- ◆ A crocodile
- ▲ A bear
- ● A wolf

Did you know?

Woolly mammoths were still alive 4,000 years ago, when the ancient Egyptian pyramids were built!

6 True or false: Woolly mammoths were smaller than African elephants.
- ◆ True
- ▲ False

7 In Australia, *Diprotodon* was a giant ...?
- ◆ Kangaroo
- ▲ Kookaburra
- ● Wombat

8 What's the name of this massive snake?
- ◆ *Titanoboa*
- ▲ *Megaboa*
- ● *Tyrranoboa*

9 The closest modern relations of *Dromornis* are ...?
- ◆ Eagles
- ▲ Ostriches
- ● Ducks

10 When did *Homo sapiens*—that's us humans—first appear on Earth?
- ◆ 60,000 years ago
- ▲ 200,000 years ago
- ● 1 million years ago

Turn to page 112 for the answers!

After the Dinosaurs
Answers

1 When the Mesozoic Era ended, which era began?

◆ The Cenozoic Era

Cenozoic means "new life." The era began 66 million years ago and it's the current period.

2 The Cenozoic Era is also called ...?

● The Age of Mammals

After the dinosaur extinction, mammals had the space to spread and soon dominated the land.

3 What is this saber-toothed cat's proper name?

◆ *Smilodon*

The biggest and best-known saber-toothed cat, fearsome-fanged *Smilodon*, first appeared in the Americas 2.5 million years ago.

4 How long were *Smilodon*'s upper canine teeth?

● 7 in (18 cm)

... and that isn't counting the roots! These curved, bladelike fangs were visible even when *Smilodon*'s mouth was closed.

5 What kind of animal was *Arctodus*?

▲ A bear

Arctodus was probably the biggest bear ever. It is sometimes called the short-faced or the bulldog bear because of its snub-nosed appearance.

6 **True or false: Woolly mammoths were smaller than African elephants.**

▲ False

These huge herbivores were much bigger than their descendants. The steppe mammoth weighed up to 11 tons (10 tonnes), twice as much as an African elephant.

7 **In Australasia, *Diprotodon* was a giant ...?**

● Wombat

Diprotodon appeared 2 million years ago and was the biggest marsupial ever. This hippo-sized herbivore only became extinct in Australia 40,000 years ago.

8 **What's the name of this massive snake?**

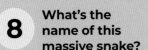

◆ *Titanoboa*

This swamp-dwelling crusher appeared 60 million years ago. It was up to 50 ft (15 m) long and weighed as much as a modern car!

9 **The closest modern relations of *Dromornis* are ...?**

● Ducks

Although huge, flightless *Dromornis* looks like an ostrich or emu, research has shown that it is more closely related to water birds like ducks.

10 **When did *Homo sapiens*—that's us humans—first appear on Earth?**

▲ 200,000 years ago

Our species evolved in Africa, then spread worldwide. Early humans hunted many of the animals on these pages and likely helped make them go extinct!

Podium!
Bronze: 1–5 correct answers
Silver: 6–8 correct answers
Gold: 9–10 correct answers

Famous Dinosaurs

Dinosaurs are still big news! Try this quiz about some of the dinosaurs, real or fictional, that have hit the headlines.

1 What was the first dinosaur skeleton to go on public display?
- ◆ Hadrosaurus
- ▲ Allosaurus
- ● Brontosaurus

2 What's the tallest dinosaur skeleton on display in a museum?
- ◆ Diplodocus
- ▲ Brachiosaurus
- ● Giraffatitan

3 What did fans nickname the *Tyrannosaurus rex* that starred in the film *Jurassic Park*?
- ◆ Rexy
- ▲ Roary
- ● Tyrone

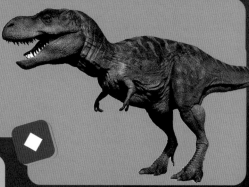

4 The Dueling Dinosaurs fossil shows which two dinosaurs fighting?
- ◆ *Triceratops* and *Tyrannosaurus rex*
- ▲ *Velociraptor* and *Diplodocus*
- ● *Spinosaurus* and *Stegosaurus*

5 In Mongolia, a recently found dinosaur nest contained how many babies?
- ◆ 3
- ▲ 10
- ● 15

6 The Natural History Museum in London, UK, has a famous *Diplodocus* called ...?

◆ Dippy
▲ Ploddy
● Dokey

7 A Netherlands museum named its *T. rex* after which famous Dutch person?

◆ Soccer player Johan Cruyff
▲ Queen Beatrix
● Artist Vincent Van Gogh

8 What's special about the *T. rex* at Fukui Dinosaur Museum, Japan?

◆ It's alive
▲ It has two tails
● It's a robot

9 What is the nickname of this *T. rex*, discovered in 1946?

◆ Tyrone
▲ Muttley
● Huxley

Did you know?

At 122 ft (37 m) long, the titanosaur on display at the American Museum of Natural History is so long that its head pokes out of the exhibition hall!

Turn to page 116 for the answers!

Famous Dinosaurs

Answers

1 **What was the first dinosaur skeleton to go on public display?**

◆ *Hadrosaurus*

Hadrosaurus foulkii, a duck-billed dinosaur, was shown to the public in 1868 in Philadelphia, Pennsylvania. It brought in massive crowds.

2 **What's the tallest dinosaur skeleton on display in a museum?**

● *Giraffatitan*

This long-necked sauropod is on show at the Natural History Museum in Berlin, Germany. It is 43.5 ft (13.27 m) high.

3 **What did fans nickname the *Tyrannosaurus rex* that starred in the film *Jurassic Park*?**

◆ Rexy

Although it wasn't given a name in the film, fans soon started referring to the dinosaur, which breaks out of its pen and goes on the rampage, as Rexy.

4 **The Dueling Dinosaurs fossil shows which two dinosaurs fighting?**

◆ *Triceratops* and *Tyrannosaurus rex*

The fossil, found in Montana in 2006, shows *Triceratops* and *T. rex* in combat.

5 — In Mongolia, a recently found dinosaur nest contained how many babies?

● 15

The *Protoceratops* babies all face the same way. They may have been shielding their faces from the sandstorm that buried them.

6 — The Natural History Museum in London, UK, has a famous *Diplodocus* called ...?

◆ Dippy

The replica fossil is 82 ft (25 m) long and was cast from a fossil found in the US around 1900.

7 — A Netherlands museum named its *T. rex* after which famous Dutch person?

▲ Queen Beatrix

The skeleton, excavated by scientists from the Naturalis Museum, was named "Trix" after Queen Beatrix, who reigned from 1980–2013.

8 — What's special about the *T. rex* at Fukui Dinosaur Museum, Japan?

● It's a robot

This life-size, lifelike animatronic roars a *Tyrannosaurus* welcome to the museum, which houses skeletons of more than 40 dinosaurs found in the area.

9 — What is the nickname of this *T. rex*, discovered in 1946?

● Huxley

The almost complete *T. rex* skeleton was found near the small settlement of Huxley, in Alberta, Canada. It is now a star exhibit at Alberta's Royal Tyrrell Museum.

Podium!

Bronze: 1–5 correct answers
Silver: 6–8 correct answers
Gold: 9–10 correct answers

Fossils

Look closer! That old lump of rock could be a fossil—a dinosaur detective's treasure trove of clues to the mysteries of Mesozoic life.

1 **What is a fossil?**
- ◆ An ancient layer of rock
- ▲ A prehistoric cave painting
- ● A preserved plant or animal

2 **What does the word "fossil" mean?**
- ◆ To keep on going
- ▲ To die out
- ● To dig

3 **Scientists who study fossils are called ...?**
- ◆ Paleontologists
- ▲ Fossologists
- ● Archaeologists

4 **Which types of body parts are most likely to become fossils?**
- ◆ Hard parts, like bones and teeth
- ▲ Soft parts, like skin and organs

5 **Which of these is a trace fossil?**
- ◆ Fossilized bone
- ▲ Fossilized poop
- ● Fossilized feathers

Did you know?

In 2016, a Chinese paleontologist found a 99-million-year-old piece of amber that contained the feathered tail of a tiny dinosaur!

6 What would NOT be in a paleontologist's field kit?
◆ Chisels
▲ Brushes
● Pneumatic drills

7 Most fossils we find are of animals that lived in:
◆ Dry deserts
▲ High mountains
● Wet places

8 Put these fossilization stages in order, earliest first:
◆ Minerals mix with the body parts
▲ The body parts turn into solid rock
● Rock builds up around a dead dinosaur

9 This fly is preserved in amber. What is amber?
◆ Ancient tree resin
▲ Precious mineral
● Volcanic glass

10 How often do scientists find a fossil of a new type of dinosaur?
◆ Every few days
▲ Every few months
● Every few years

Turn to page 120 for the answers!

Fossils
Answers

1 **What is a fossil?**
- A preserved plant or animal

When some dinosaurs died, they ended up buried in sediment. This kept them—or parts of them—from rotting away, and eventually the remains turned to rock.

2 **What does the word "fossil" mean?**
- To dig

The Latin word *fosso* means "to dig." Dinosaur remains are often buried deep underground, so digging is the only way to discover them.

3 **Scientists who study fossils are called …?**
- ◆ Paleontologists

The word was created from two Greek words meaning "ancient" and "study of things."

4 **Which types of body parts are most likely to become fossils?**
- ◆ Hard parts, like bones and teeth

Hard body parts rot away more slowly, so they are more likely to be covered by sediment before they disappear.

5 **Which of these is a trace fossil?**
- ▲ Fossilized poop

Trace fossils are not dinosaurs' body parts; instead, they are remains of the things they left behind, such as footprints and poop.

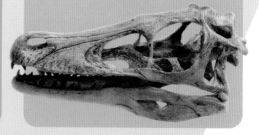

6
What would NOT be in a paleontologist's field kit?

● Pneumatic drills

Digging up dinosaurs is slow, careful work. Using a big drill would risk damaging the remains, so paleontologists use precision tools to uncover the treasures.

7
Most fossils we find are of animals that lived in:

● Wet places

Near the coast, sand and mud are more likely to quickly cover a dead creature. That's why many more fossils of marine reptiles have been found than fossils of dinosaurs.

8
Put these fossilization stage in order, earliest first:

● Rock builds up around a dead dinosaur

◆ Minerals mix with the body parts

▲ The body parts turn into solid rock

Millions of years later, the deeply buried animal can be brought closer to the surface by Earth movements or by weather or waves eroding the surrounding rocks.

9
This fly is preserved in amber. What is amber?

◆ Ancient tree resin

Some trees produce a sticky liquid called resin to protect themselves. Small animals can get trapped in the resin, which then sets hard—and lasts for millions of years!

10
How often do scientists find a fossil of a new type of dinosaur?

◆ Every few days

Dinosaurs were around for an extremely long time—170 million years or so—and there are still many species left for us to discover.

Podium!

Bronze: 1–5 correct answers

Silver: 6–8 correct answers

Gold: 9–10 correct answers

Modern Survivors

Some of our animals are older than they look! These living fossils have hardly changed since they shared Earth with the dinosaurs.

1 The caiman and the huge *Deinosuchus* are both members of which family?

◆ Raptors
▲ Crocodylomorphs
● Tyrannosaurs

2 Which modern crocodilian has the narrowest snout?

◆ Alligator
▲ Gharial
● Crocodile

Did you know?

Modern birds are the only dinosaurs still alive today, but many of them have developed a talent that only a few dinosaurs ever had—they can fly!

3 True or false: Today's cow sharks are closely related to prehistoric sharks.

◆ True
▲ False

4 Can you identify this bird, which has a prehistoric secret?

◆ Pigeon
▲ Hoatzin
● Parrot

5 When did the first velvet worm appear on Earth?
◆ 540 million years ago
▲ 310 million years ago
● 160 million years ago

6 How long have dragonflies been on Earth?
◆ 600 million years
▲ 320 million years
● 250 million years

7 Which parasite first evolved to live on feathered dinosaurs?
◆ Feather worm
▲ Feather louse
● Feather flea

8 True or false: Horsetail plants are the same size today as they were in prehistoric times.
◆ True
▲ False

9 The extinct fish *Coelacanth* was rediscovered in ...?
◆ 1838
▲ 1938
● 2018

Scan the QR code for a Kahoot! about modern survivors.

Turn to page 124 for the answers!

Modern Survivors
Answers

1 **The caiman and the huge *Deinosuchus* are both members of which family?**

▲ Crocodylomorphs

Deinosuchus is now extinct, but today's crocodylomorphs include crocodiles, caimans, gharials, and alligators.

2 **Which modern crocodilian has the narrowest snout?**

▲ Gharial

This Asian reptile hunts in rivers. Its long, thin jaws are lined with 110 teeth, perfect for grabbing and gripping slippery, scaly prey.

3 **True or false: Today's cow sharks are closely related to prehistoric sharks.**

◆ True

Along with frilled sharks, cow sharks form the most ancient branch of the shark family. They appeared about 200 million years ago.

4 **Can you identify this bird, which has a prehistoric secret?**

▲ *Hoatzin*

Like their birdlike dinosaur distant relatives, *Hoatzin* chicks have claws halfway along their wings. These help the chicks cling to branches.

5 When did the first velvet worm appear on Earth?

◆ 540 million years ago

These soft-bodied, centipedelike worms live on the floor of tropical rainforests. They kill their prey with jets of poisonous slime!

6 How long have dragonflies been on Earth?

▲ 320 million years

The first dragonflylike insects were called griffenflies. One type, called *Meganeuropsis permiana*, is thought to be the largest insect ever!

7 Which parasite first evolved to live on feathered dinosaurs?

▲ Feather louse

These tiny, wingless insects evolved around 130 million years ago. They're still chewing on birds' feathers today.

8 True or false: Horsetail plants are the same size today as they were in prehistoric times.

▲ False

Today, horsetails grow to about 3.3 ft (1 m) tall. The Carboniferous versions could reach 165 ft (50 m)!

9 The extinct fish *Coelacanth* was rediscovered in ...?

▲ 1938

Scientists thought that *Coelacanth* became extinct along with the dinosaurs—until a fisherman in South Africa caught a live one in his net!

Podium!

Bronze: 1–5 correct answers

Silver: 6–8 correct answers

Gold: 9–10 correct answers

Glossary

Arthropods
A group of animals, including insects, that have a hard outer skeleton, jointed legs, and a segmented body.

Carnivore
An animal that eats only meat.

Cretaceous Period
The third period of the Mesozoic Era, from 145–66 million years ago.

Fossilization
The process by which a living thing becomes a fossil, preserved in rock.

Habitat
A specific place in which an animal or plant lives.

Herbivore
An animal that eats only plants.

Jurassic Period
The second period of the Mesozoic Era, from 201–145 million years ago.

Mammals
Warm-blooded, furry, or hairy animals that feed milk to their young.

Mesozoic Era
The Triassic, Jurassic, and Cretaceous Periods together.

Meteor
A lump of rock that falls from space and burns up as it enters Earth's atmosphere.

Migrate
Move from one place to another to find food, a mate, or better weather.

Predator
An animal that survives by hunting and eating other animals.

Prehistoric
Ancient time before history was officially recorded.

Reptiles
Cold-blooded, scaly-skinned animals that mostly reproduce by laying eggs.

Triassic Period
The first period of the Mesozoic Era, from 252–201 million years ago.

Picture Credits

The publisher would like to thank the following for their kind permission to reproduce their photographs:

(Key: a-above; b-below/bottom; c-center; f-far; l-left; r-right; t-top)

2 Dorling Kindersley: Natural History Museum, London (cra). **Science Photo Library:** Julius T Csotonyi (bl). **3 Shutterstock.com:** lego 19861111 (clb). **4 123RF.com:** Mark Turner (cr, bl). **5 Dorling Kindersley:** Jon Hughes (cra). **7 Dorling Kindersley:** Natural History Museum, London (cla). **Dreamstime.com:** Mark Turner (cra). **8 Dorling Kindersley:** James Kuether (br). **10 Dorling Kindersley:** James Kuether (cra). **11 Dorling Kindersley:** Natural History Museum, London (tr). **13 Dorling Kindersley:** Natural History Museum, London (cra). **19 Getty Images:** leonello (tr). **20 Dorling Kindersley:** Natural History Museum, London (br). **22 Dorling Kindersley:** Natural History Museum, London (bc). **23 Dorling Kindersley:** Courtesy of Dorset Dinosaur Museum (cra). **26 Dorling Kindersley:** James Kuether (c). **27 123RF.com:** Ian Dikhtiar (tr). **Getty Images:** Mohamad Haghani / Stocktrek Images (cla). **28 Fotolia:** DM7 (cl). **29 123RF.com:** albertus engbers (bl). **Dreamstime.com:** Dario Lo Presti (tr). **30 123RF.com:** Michael Rosskothen (cr). **31 Dorling Kindersley:** Senckenberg Gesellschaft Fuer Naturforschung Museum (ca). **32 Dreamstime.com:** Elena Duvernay (br). **34 Dorling Kindersley:** Jon Hughes (cra). **35 Dreamstime.com:** David Havel (cra). **36 Dreamstime.com:** Elena Duvernay (crb). **37 Dreamstime.com:** David Havel (clb). **39 Dorling Kindersley:** Roby Braun (c); Natural History Museum, London (tr). **42 123RF.com:** Corey A Ford (cl). **43 123RF.com:** leonello calvetti (cr). **44 Getty Images / iStock:** milehightraveler (br)**. 47 Dorling Kindersley:** Natural History Museum, London (cl). **Dreamstime.com:** Mr1805 (cr). **48 Dorling Kindersley:** James Kuether (br). **50 Dorling Kindersley:** Senckenberg Gesellschaft Fuer Naturforschung Museum (cr). **51 123RF.com:** Michael Rosskothen (cra). **52 123RF.com:** Elena Duvernay (cr). **53 123RF.com:** Michael Rosskothen (cla). **54 Dorling Kindersley:** Trustees of the Natural History Museum, London (crb). **55 Shutterstock.com:** Daniel Eskridge (clb). **56 Dorling Kindersley:** Natural History Museum, London (cra). **57 Dreamstime.com:** S100apm (tr). **60 Dorling Kindersley:** Natural History Museum, London (cra). **61 Science Photo Library:** Julius T Csotonyi (cl). **Shutterstock.com:** Daniel Eskridge (tr). **62 Dreamstime.com:** Andreas Meyer (cr). **63 Dorling Kindersley:** Bristol City Museum and Art Gallery (tr). **Dreamstime.com:** Dmytro Strelbytskyy (bl). **64 123RF.com:** Corey A Ford (br). **65 123RF.com:** Mark Turner (cra). **66 123RF.com:** Corey A Ford (cra, bl). **67 123RF.com:** Corey A Ford **(clb). Dreamstime.com:** Mr1805 (tr). **69 123RF.com:** Corey A Ford (bl). **Dorling Kindersley:** Jon Hughes (tr). **70-71 123RF.com:** Mark Turner (bc). **71 Dorling Kindersley:** Royal Tyrrell Museum of Palaeontology, Alberta, Canada (clb). **Dreamstime.com:** Mr1805 (cr). **72 123RF.com:** Elena Duvernay (crb). **Dorling Kindersley:** American Museum of Natural History (cra). **73 Dreamstime.com:** Mr1805 (cra). **74 Dreamstime.com:** Mr1805 (cr). **75 123RF.com:** Valentyna Chukhlyebova (cr). **77 Getty Images / iStock:** CoreyFord (tr). **79 Dorling Kindersley:** Hunterian Museum University of Glasgow (tr). **Shutterstock.com:** Kathy Hutchins (br). **80 Dreamstime.com:** Jaroslaw Grudzinski / Jarek78 (br). **82 Dreamstime.com:** Mr1805 (crb). **83 123RF.com:** Mark Turner (crb). **Dorling Kindersley:** Senckenberg Gesellschaft Fuer Naturforschung Museum (cr). **84 123RF.com:** Elena Duvernay (clb). **85 Getty Images /**
iStock: dottedhippo (tr). **86 123RF.com:** Suwat wongkham (cr). **Dorling Kindersley:** Peter Minister (br). **89 Dorling Kindersley:** James Kuether (cr). **90 123RF.com:** alexeykonovalenko (clb). **Dorling Kindersley:** Carnegie Museum of Natural History, Pittsburgh (br). **91 123RF.com:** Corey A Ford (clb). **93 Dorling Kindersley:** Courtesy of Dorset Dinosaur Museum (c); James Kuether (cra). **94 123RF.com:** Corey A Ford (crb). **Dreamstime.com:** Elena Duvernay (cra). **95 Dreamstime.com:** Mr1805 (cl). **96 123RF.com:** Mark Turner (br). **97 Dorling Kindersley:** James Kuether (tr); Royal Tyrrell Museum of Palaeontology, Alberta, Canada (cr). **98 Dorling Kindersley:** American Museum of Natural History (cr); Courtesy of Dorset Dinosaur Museum (cl). **99 Dorling Kindersley:** Courtesy of Dorset Dinosaur Museum (bc). **Dreamstime.com:** Corey A Ford (cra). **100 Dorling Kindersley:** Peter Minister (bl). **103 123RF.com:** Alexandr Pakhnyushchyy / alekss (clb). **106 Dreamstime.com:** Satori13 (cra). **107 Dreamstime.com:** mopic (cla). **109 Alamy Stock Photo:** Nobumichi Tamura / Stocktrek Images (bl). **110 Dorling Kindersley:** James Kuether (crb). **111 123RF.com:** Michael Rosskothen / miro3d (clb). **Dorling Kindersley:** Royal British Columbia Museum, Victoria, Canada (tr). **Science Photo Library:** Ja Chirinos (cr). **112 Dorling Kindersley:** James Kuether (bl). **114 Dorling Kindersley:** Peter Minister (crb). **115 Alamy Stock Photo:** Robert McGouey (clb). **116 Shutterstock.com:** Computer Earth (br). **117 Shutterstock.com:** lego 19861111 (clb). **118 Getty Images / iStock:** benedek (cra). **119 Dorling Kindersley:** Natural History Museum (bl). **Getty Images / iStock:** Userba011d64_201 (cr). **120 Getty Images / iStock:** Crazytang (br). **121 Dorling Kindersley:** Natural History Museum, London (cla). **122 Dreamstime.com:** Joan Egert / Physi28 (br). **123 Getty Images / iStock:** Christophe Sirabella (clb). **124 Dreamstime.com:** Pindiyath100 (cr). **126 Dorling Kindersley:** Peter Minister (br). **127 123RF.com:** Suwat wongkham (br). **Dorling Kindersley:** Natural History Museum, London (tr). **128 Dorling Kindersley:** Jon Hughes (tr)

Cover images: *Front: Alamy Stock Photo: Mohamad Haghani br;* **Dorling Kindersley:** *Tim Parmenter / Natural History Museum, London clb;* **Getty Images /** iStock: *Crazytang tr; Back:* **123RF.com:** *leonello calvetti tr, Mark Turner cl;* **Dorling Kindersley:** *Jon Hughes tl*

All other images © Dorling Kindersley

Dorling Kindersley would like to thank Morten Versvik, Ritesh Maisuria, Perla P. Pinto, Francisco Bembibre, and Craig Narveson at Kahoot! DK also thanks the author Rona Skene, consultant Dr. Dean Lomax for fact checking, and Julia March for proofreading.

DK | Penguin Random House

DK LONDON

Senior Editor Laura Palosuo
Senior Art Editor Anna Formanek
Editor Elizabeth Cook
Senior US Editor Kayla Dugger
Executive US Editor Lori Cates Hand
Designer Samantha Richiardi
Consultant Dr. Dean Lomax
Managing Editor Paula Regan
Managing Art Editor Jo Connor
Managing Director Mark Searle
Senior Production Editor Jennifer Murray
Senior Production Controller Lloyd Robertson
Jacket Designers James McKeag and Samantha Richiardi
Written by Rona Skene

First American Edition, 2004
Published in the United States by DK Publishing,
a division of Penguin Random House LLC
1745 Broadway, 20th Floor, New York, NY 10019

20 21 22 23 24 10 9 8 7 6 5 4 3 2 1
001–340613–Jun/2024

A catalog record for this book
is available from the Library of Congress.
ISBN 978-0-7440-9893-8

Printed and bound in China

www.dk.com
www.kahoot.com
create.kahoot.it/profiles/dk-learning-uk

MIX
Paper | Supporting
responsible forestry
FSC™ C018179

This book was made with Forest
Stewardship Council™ certified
paper—one small step in DK's
commitment to a sustainable future.
Learn more at
www.dk.com/uk/information/sustainability